Tucker Goes to Kindergarten

Story by
Lea Bartch

Illustrated by
Kaylea J. Mangrum

ISBN: 9780988300965

Foreword

Lea Bartch

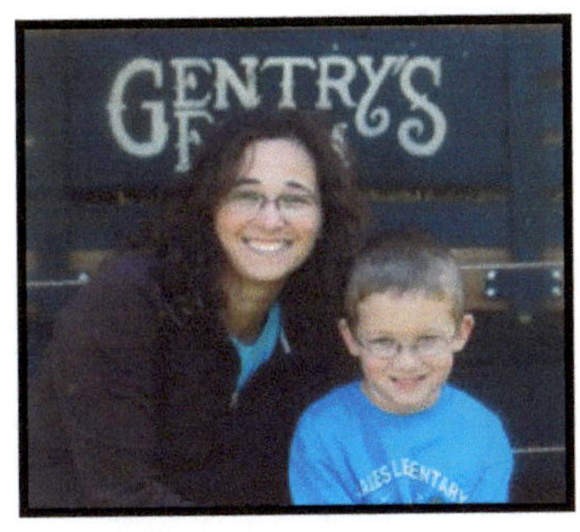

Lea Bartch began her teaching career at the age of 5 with her imaginary students and leftover ditto sheets. Her professional career continued after graduating with a Masters in Education from Harding University in 1995. She is furthering her education by mothering three of her own children and teaching a classroom of kindergarten people in Murfreesboro, Tennessee. Lea is passionate about the education of children. She believes learning never ceases. As the story demonstrates, there is something for everyone.

Kaylea J. Mangrum

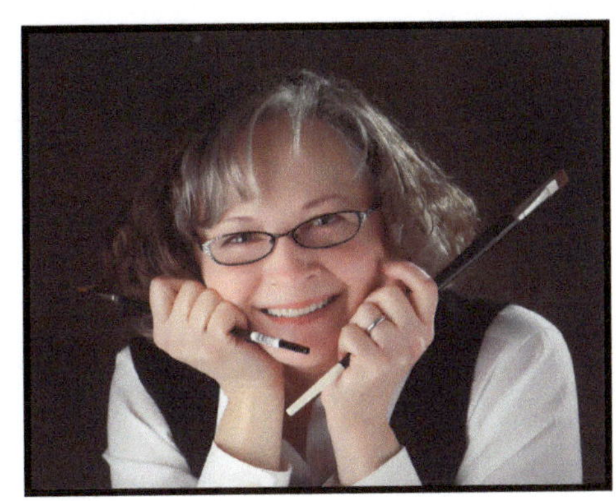

When I was young I loved to draw. But as I grew, drawing became too difficult. I finally stopped completely until my children started asking me to draw for them. I started volunteering at school with art projects. When my last child graduated from high school, the principal of his school ask me to start an art program for grades K-4 thru 6th grade.

As a self-taught artist, this was quite an undertaking. How could I break down the steps of drawing? I was determined to find steps that all ages could understand. After a lot of searching, I finally found my own technique.

Three lines were all I needed. Every picture, letter, or number could be drawn or written with these three lines. It was important to me that the lines could be described to and understood by a 3 or 4 year old child. That is how I came up with frog hops. All children like little frogs and know that a frog hops.

The other two lines were a smile (upward curve) and a straight line. Add dots in the right place and anyone can make a picture.

In 2006 I was added to a team at Special Kids to work with children with special needs. This was a new art therapy program. The children at Special Kids responded well to the frog hops; therefore, I continue to build on the frog hop foundation.

Dedication

I dedicate this book to all teachers who help and encourage students to dream, and to make those dreams become realities.

Acknowledgements

To Mrs. Hookstra, Tucker's kindergarten teacher, thank you for making his first year of school a special one, and for giving me suggestions and encouragement when I needed it.

To Phillip, my youngest son, for the final work in the creation of this book.

Most of all I thank God for making it all possible and for giving me four sweet grand-children. Tucker is one of them.

A note to parents or teachers:
If you are working with a child with special needs or a beginner,
you will have to draw the dots and say the words needed.

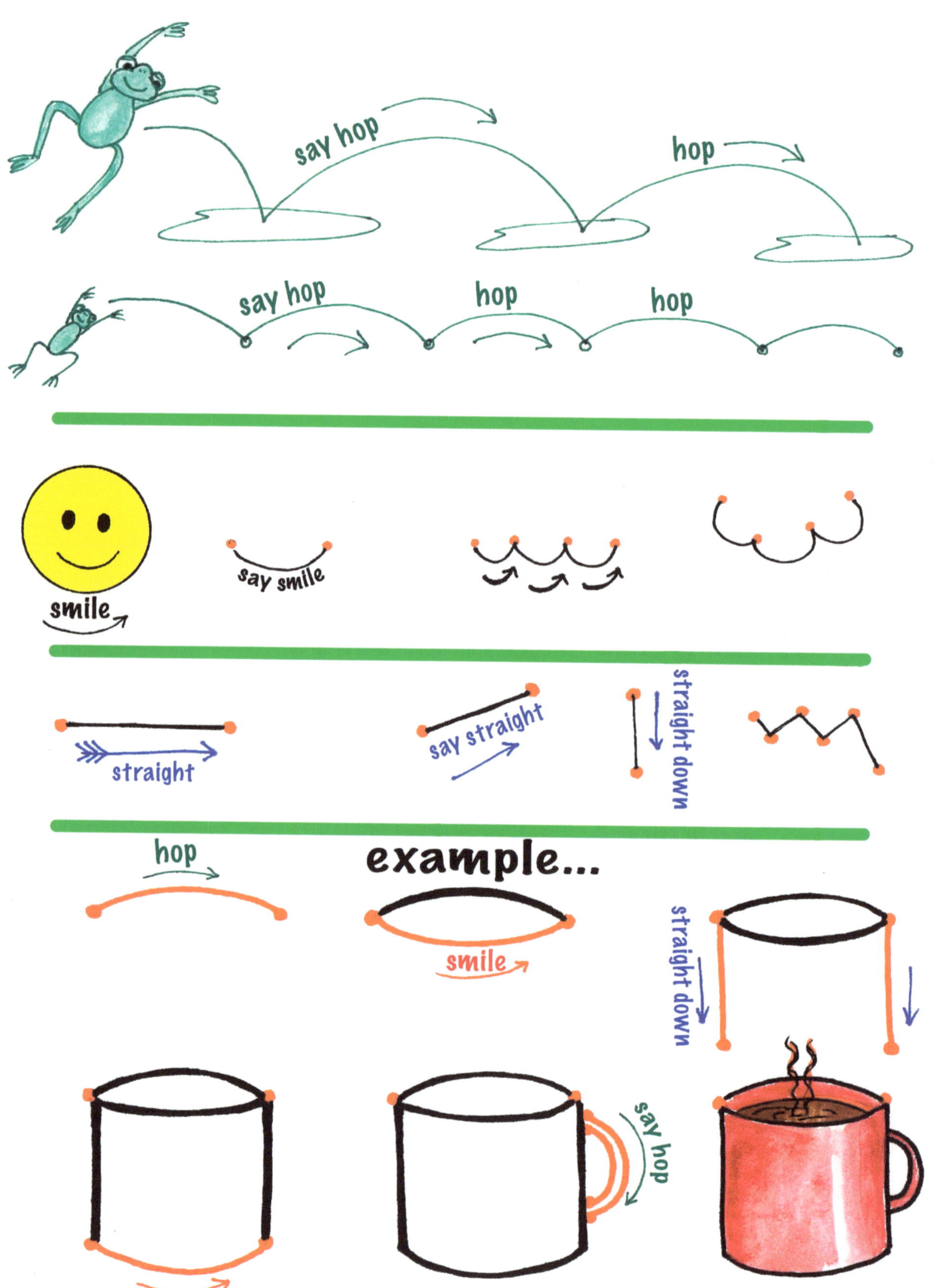

say hop
hop
say hop
hop
hop
smile
say smile
straight
say straight
straight down
hop
example...
smile
straight down
say hop

Table of Contents

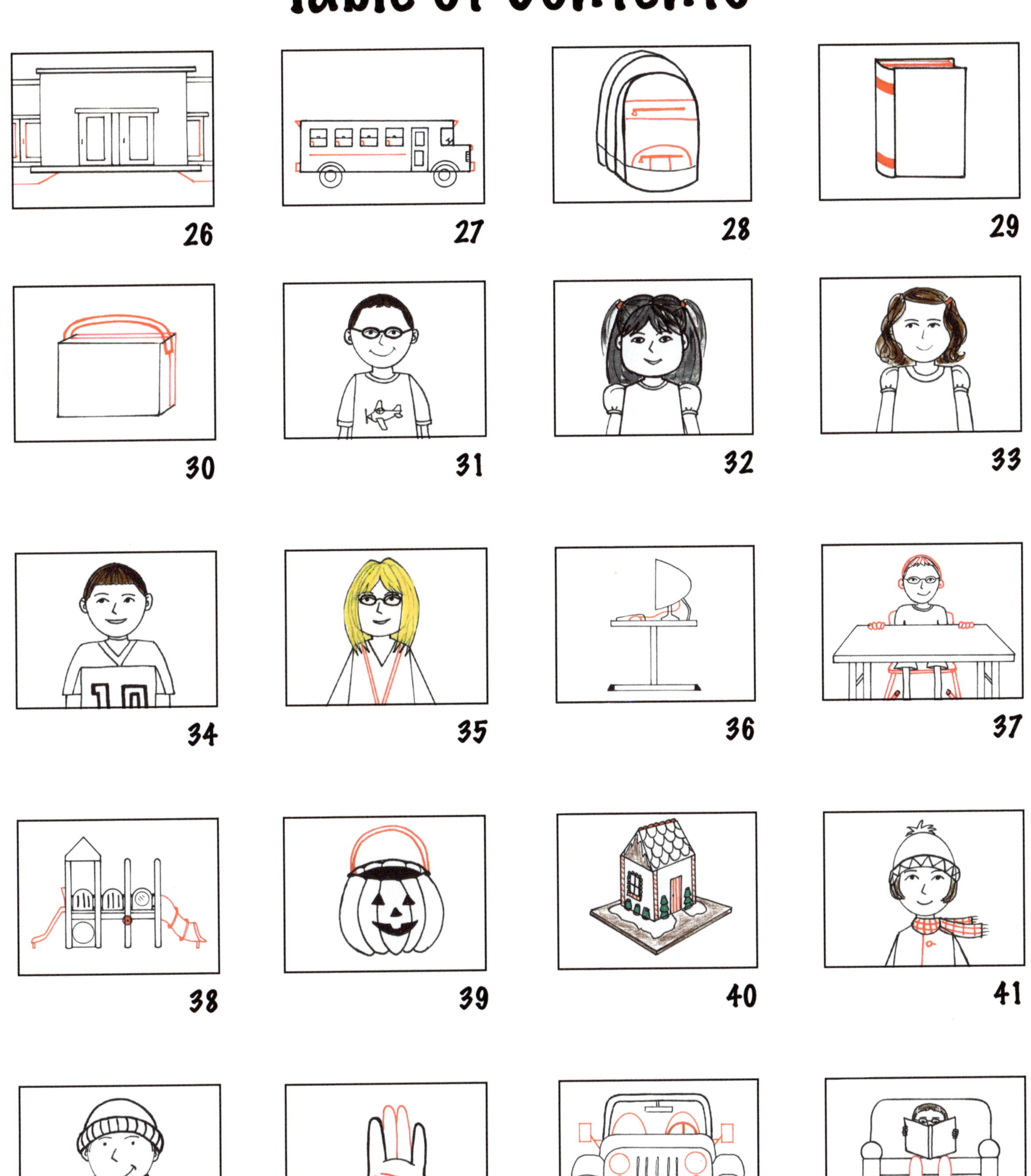

Look at me.

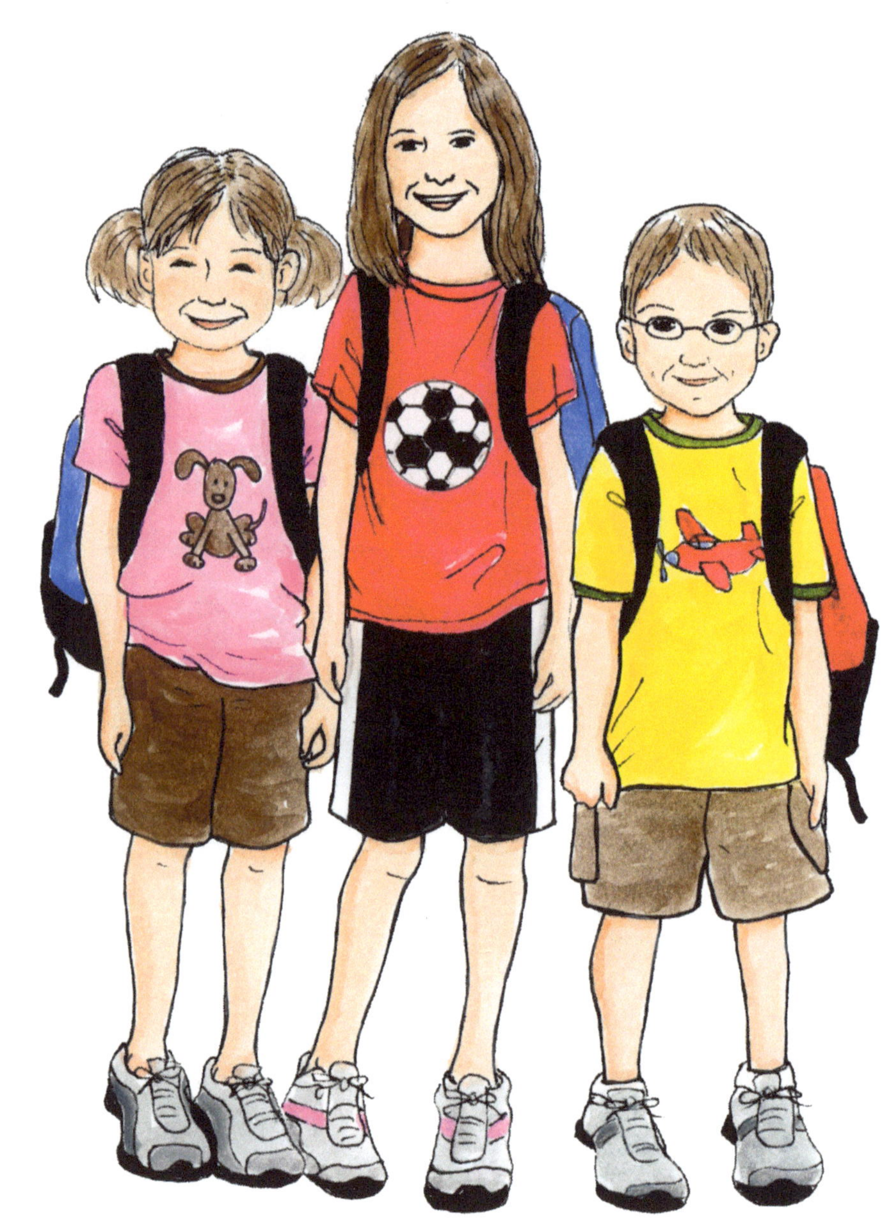

Last year, I went to school with my big sisters. I felt excited and nervous.

Look at my supplies.

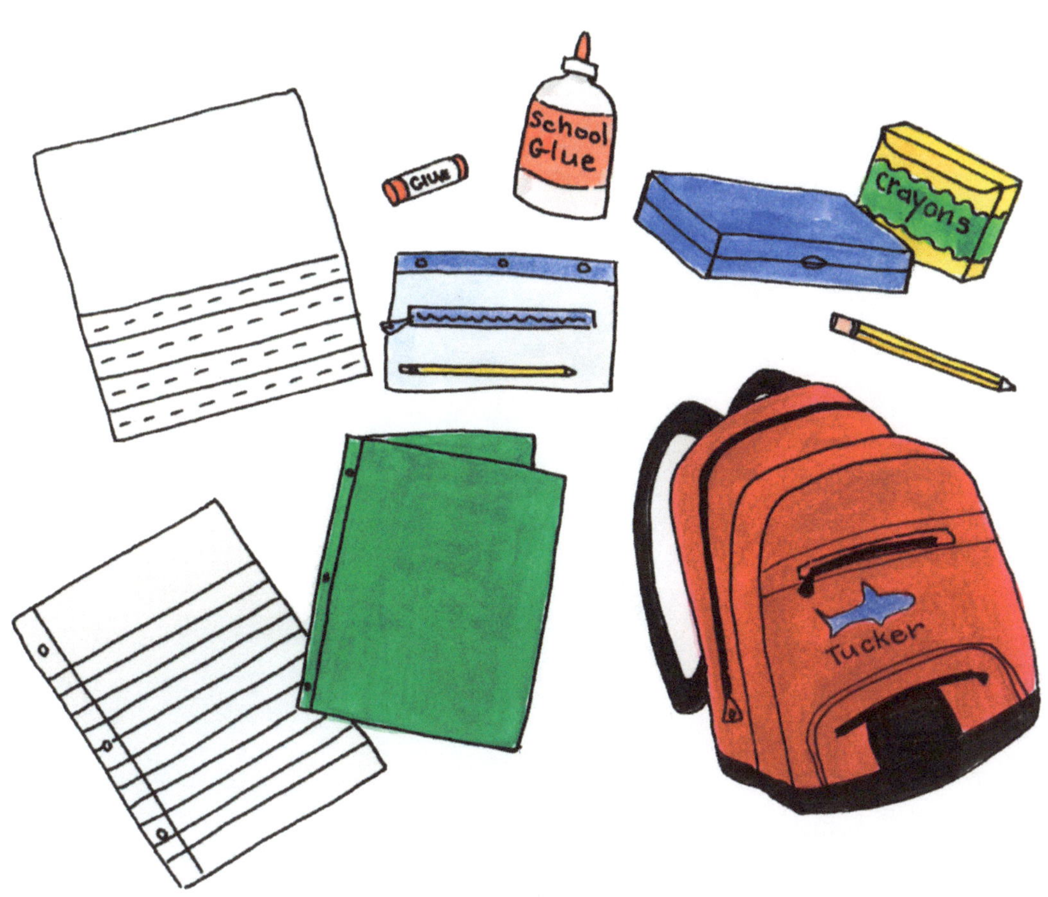

I bought glue, pencils, scissors, and a new backpack. I couldn't wait to use all of my new supplies.

Look at me walk to class.

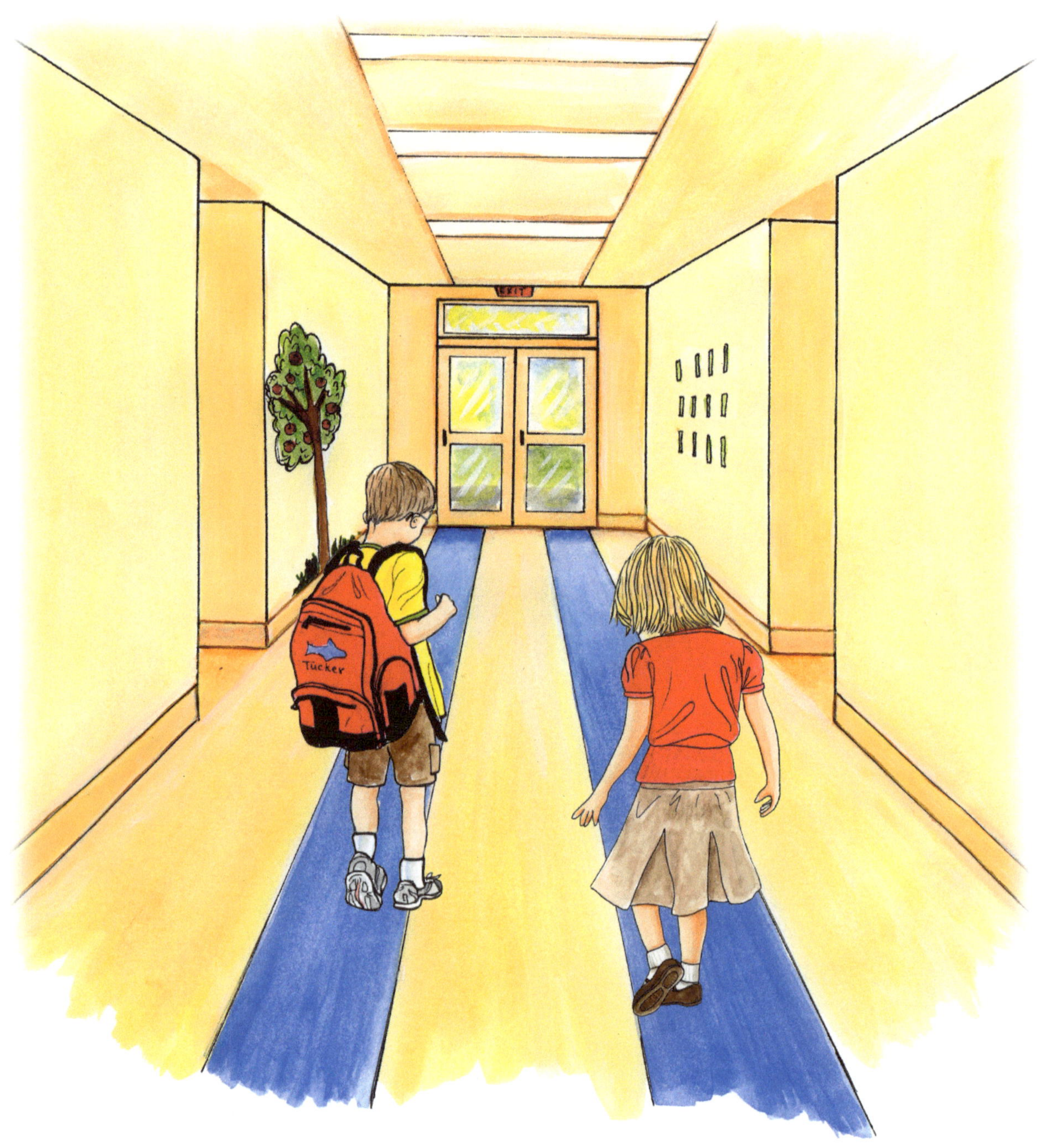

I told mom on the first day of school, "I can do this all by myself." I was born ready for kindergarten. My mom cried a little because she wasn't ready.

Here is my teacher.

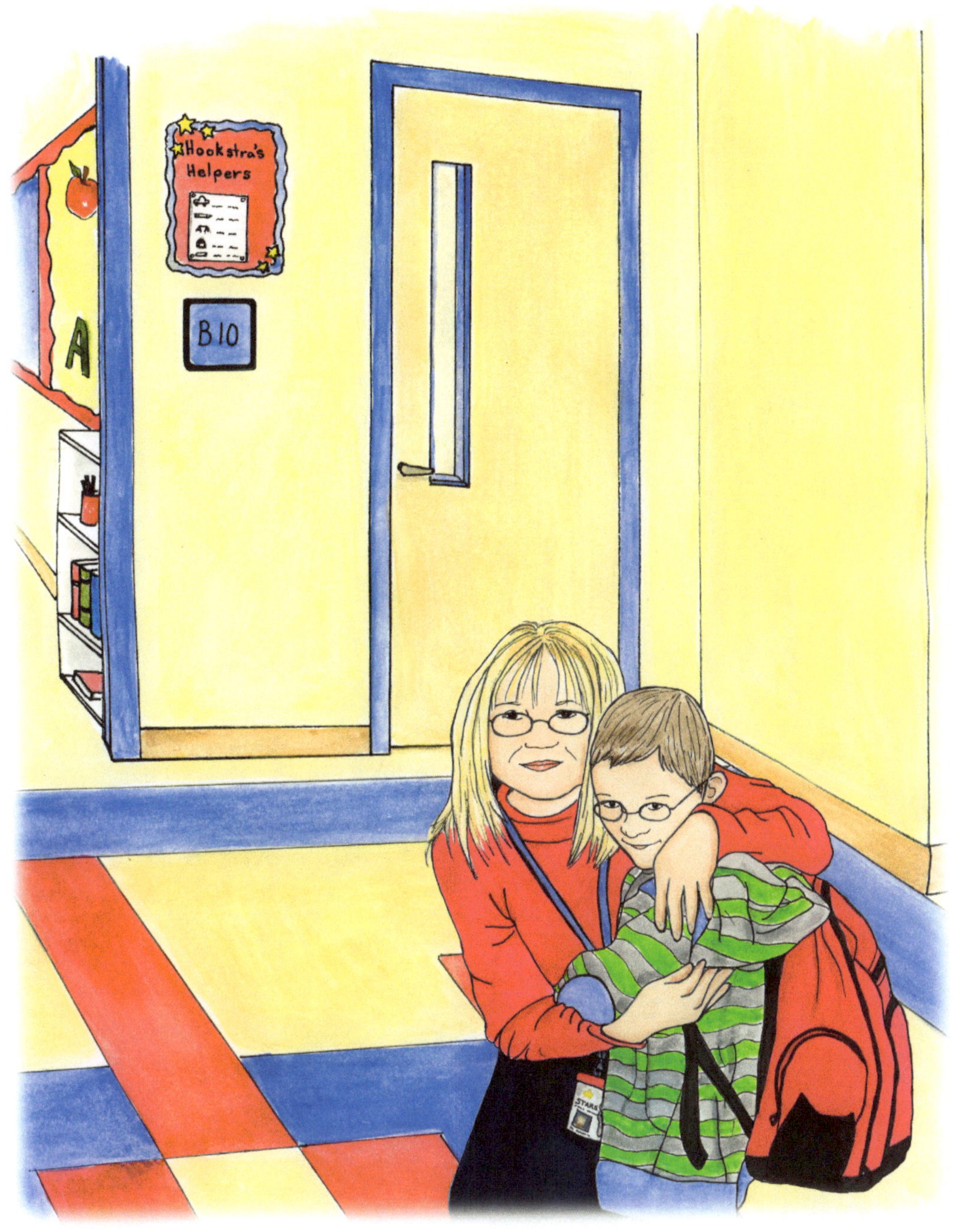

Every morning Mrs. Hookstra waited at the door for me. She was always happy to see me. We liked each other a lot!

Here is my cubby.

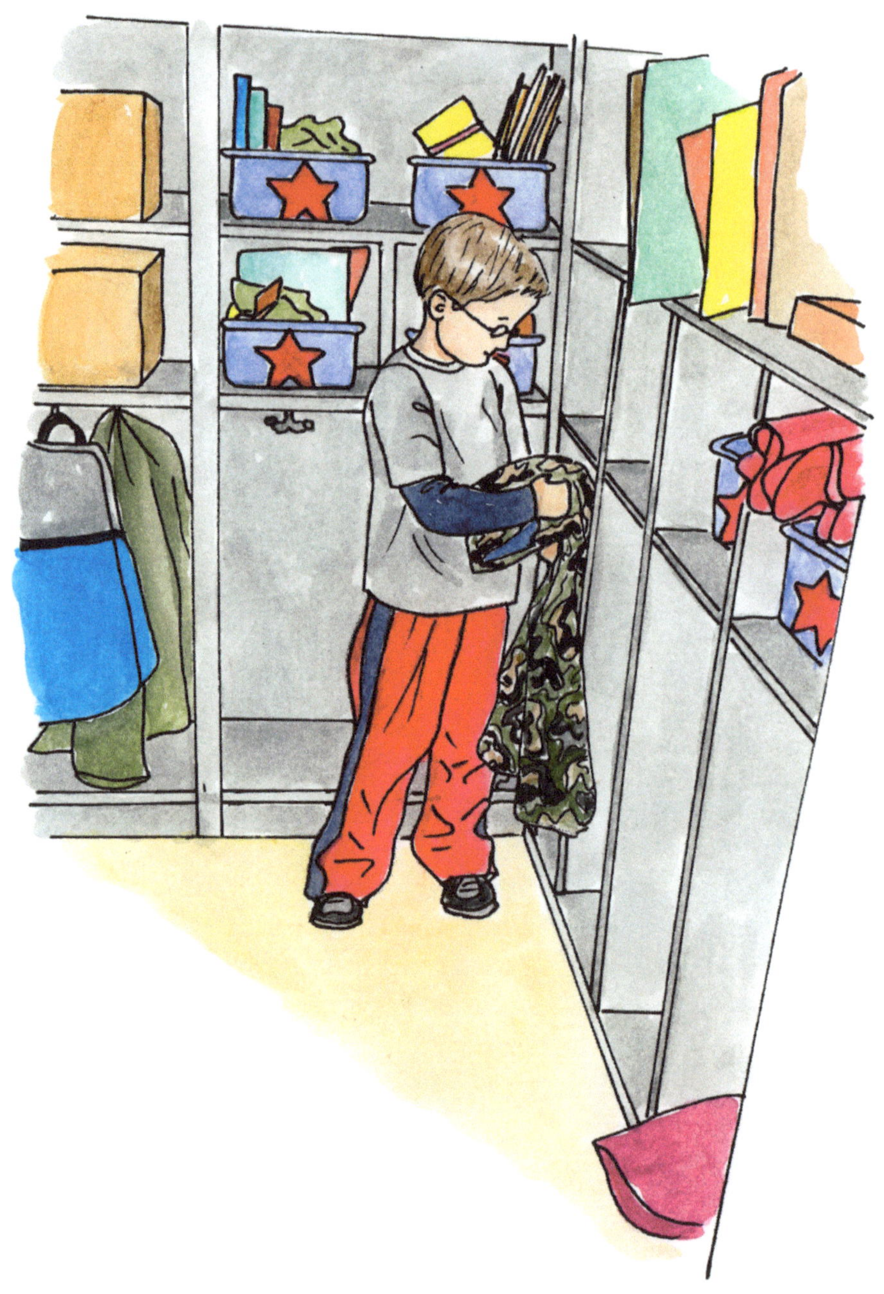

Mrs. Hookstra taught us how to put our things away. She also taught us how to raise our hands, be kind to others, and turn bad situations into good ones!

Here is my desk.

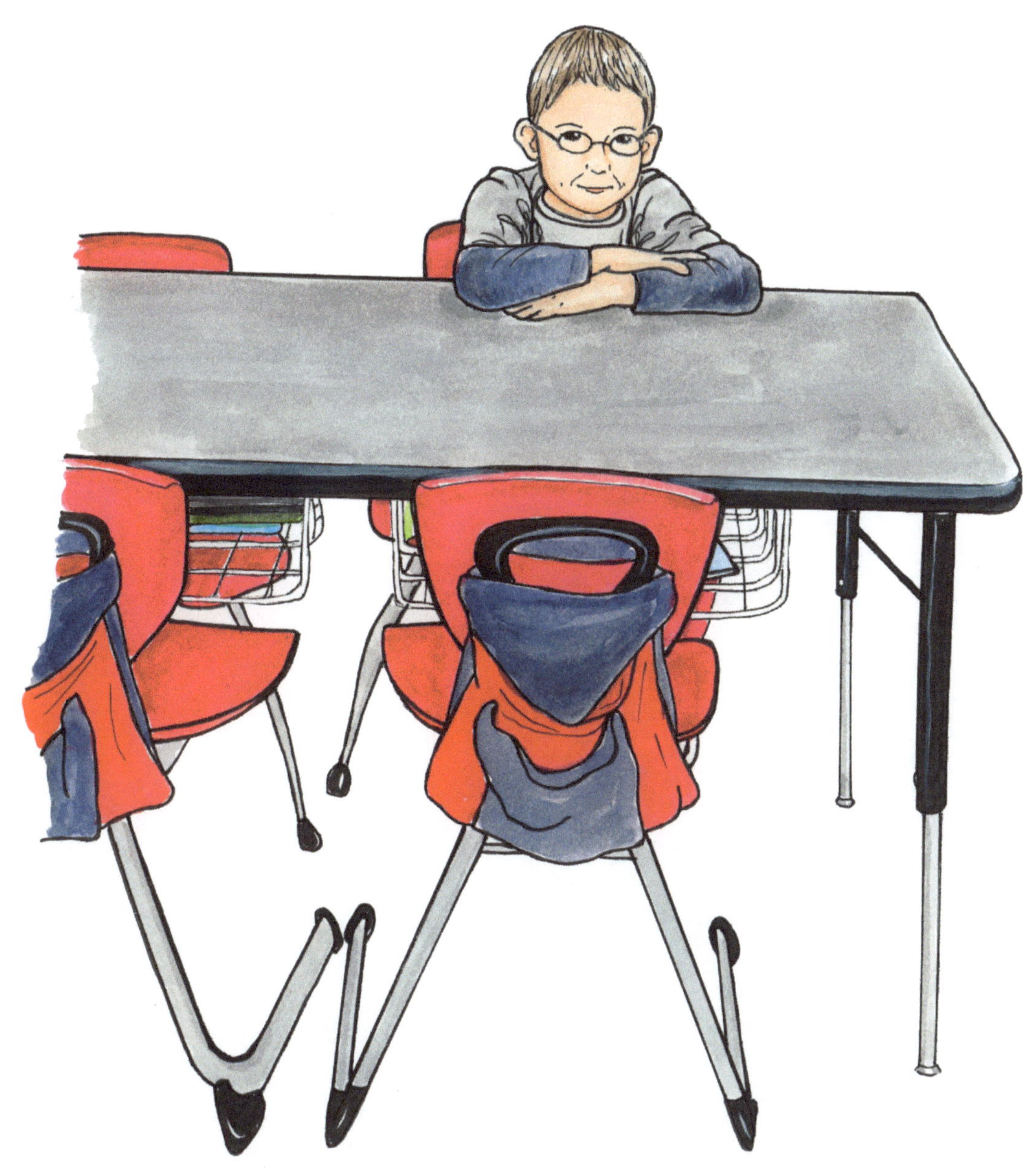

I had my very own desk. Each morning Mrs. Hookstra liked us to be
ready so we could learn. She said listening helps you learn, too. I
didn't want to miss anything, so I **ALWAYS** listened. (Well, sometimes
I forgot to listen.)

See us talk on the carpet?

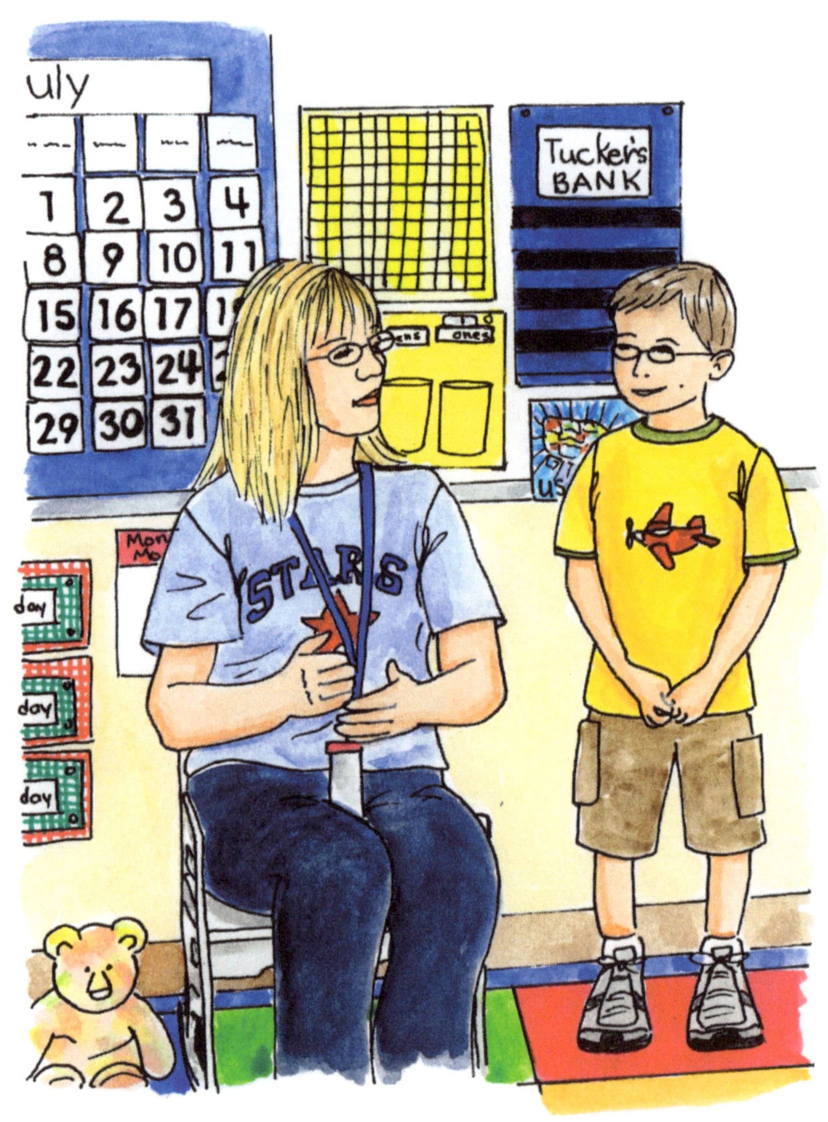

I loved to talk with my classmates. Each morning we used sign language to say, "I am loved. I am accepted. And I am glad to be me." Mrs. Hookstra also taught us how to make other friends feel loved and accepted. We gave compliments to each other.

Here is our calendar.

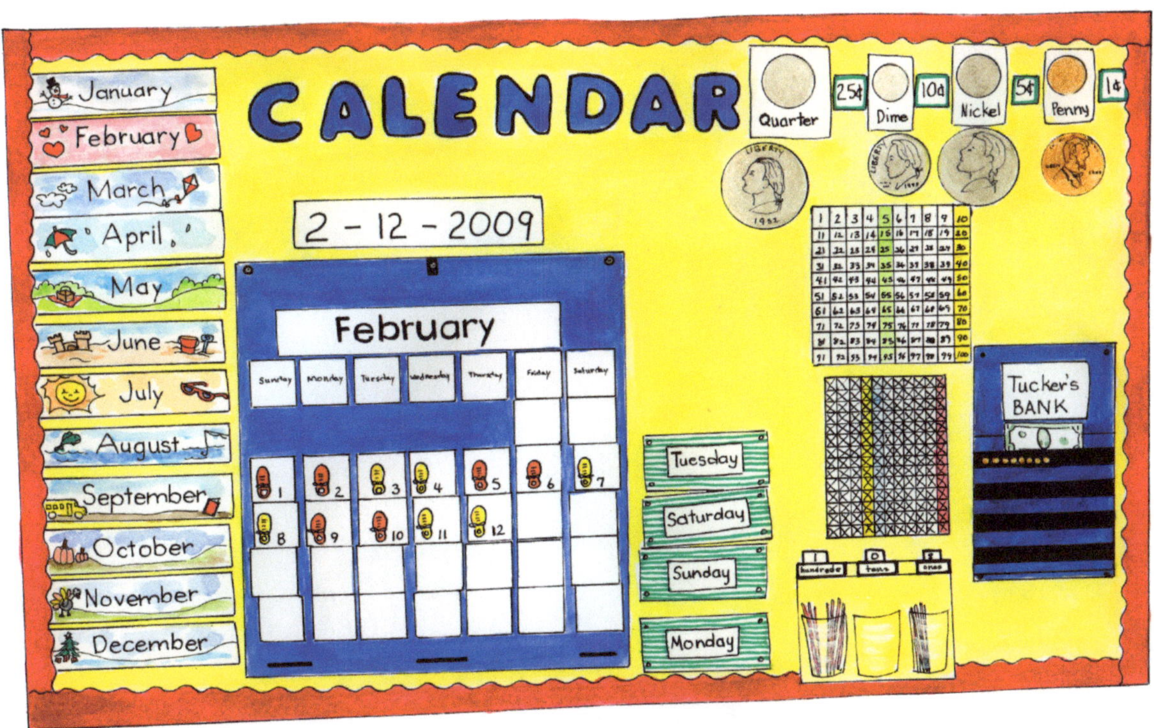

We also sat on the carpet to learn about math! Math is important, and we will use our math brains for the rest of our lives. Did you know a caldendar measures time? Do you know what pattern comes next? I do, because I learned that in kindergarten.

See us read a book?

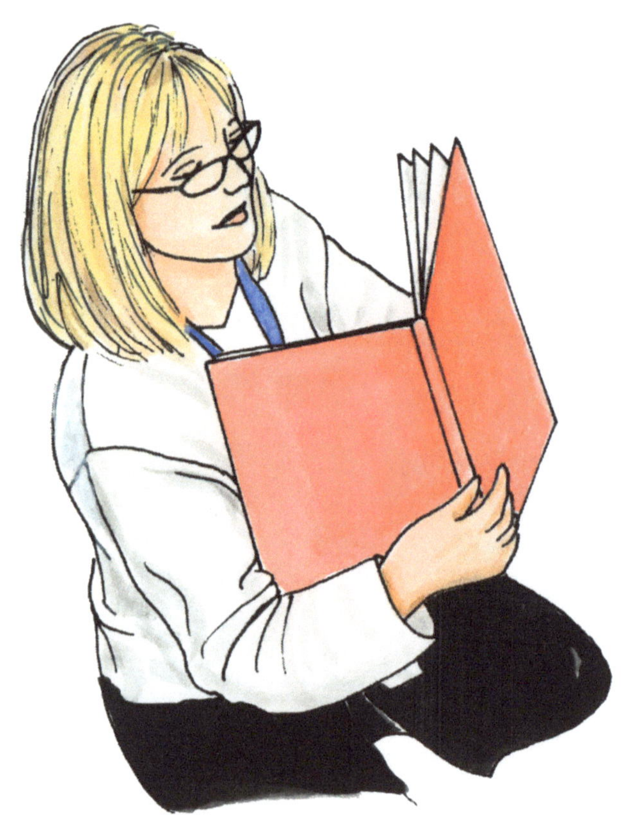

I learned to read in kindergarten! Did you know words are made of letters? Each letter makes a sound. Putting words together make sentences. I also learned that words have families, just like me. I loved hearing my teacher read to me.

We went to lunch!

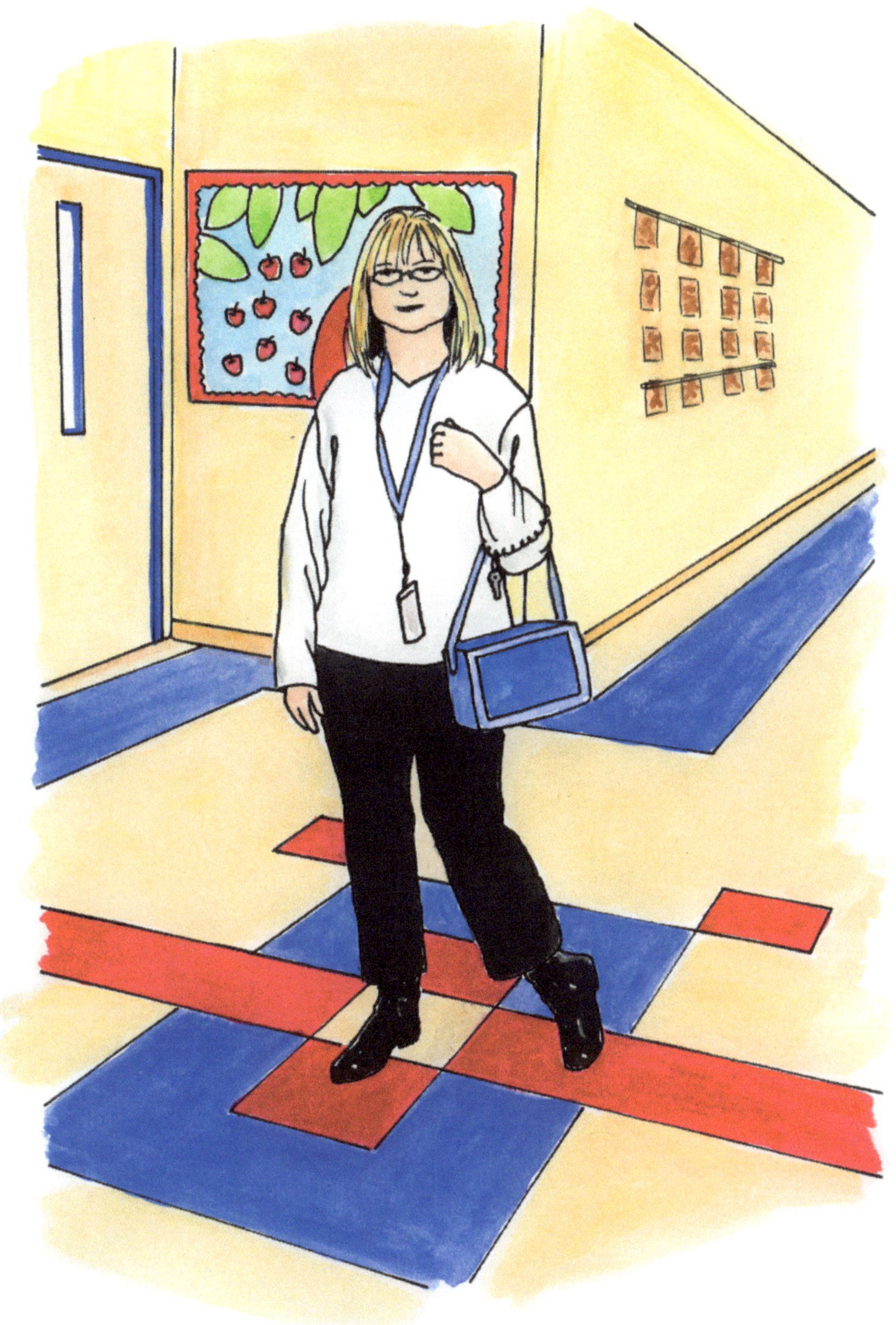

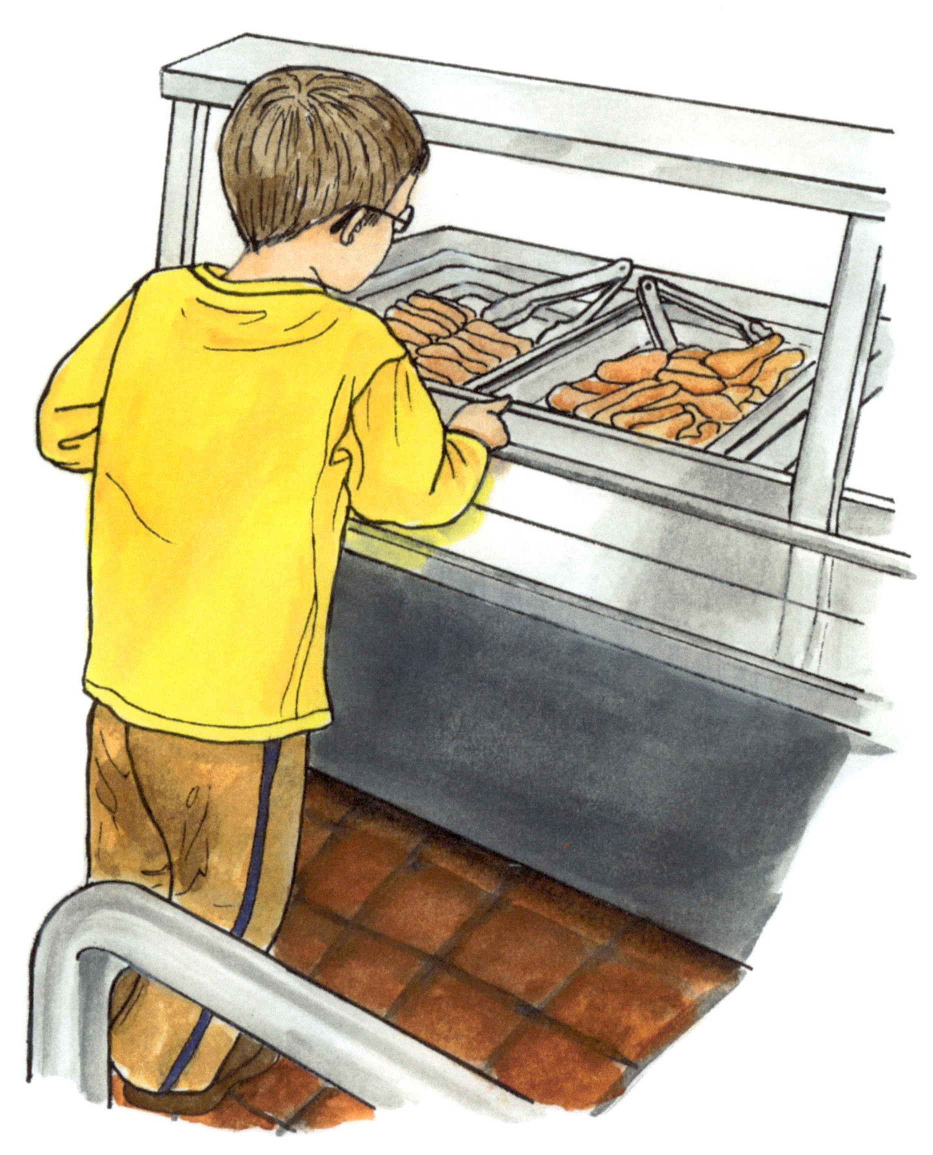

YUM! Lunch was a great part of my day. I could bring a lunch from home or buy a hot lunch. My favorite hot lunch was bacon cheeseburgers. Sometimes I got to buy ice cream.

We went to centers.

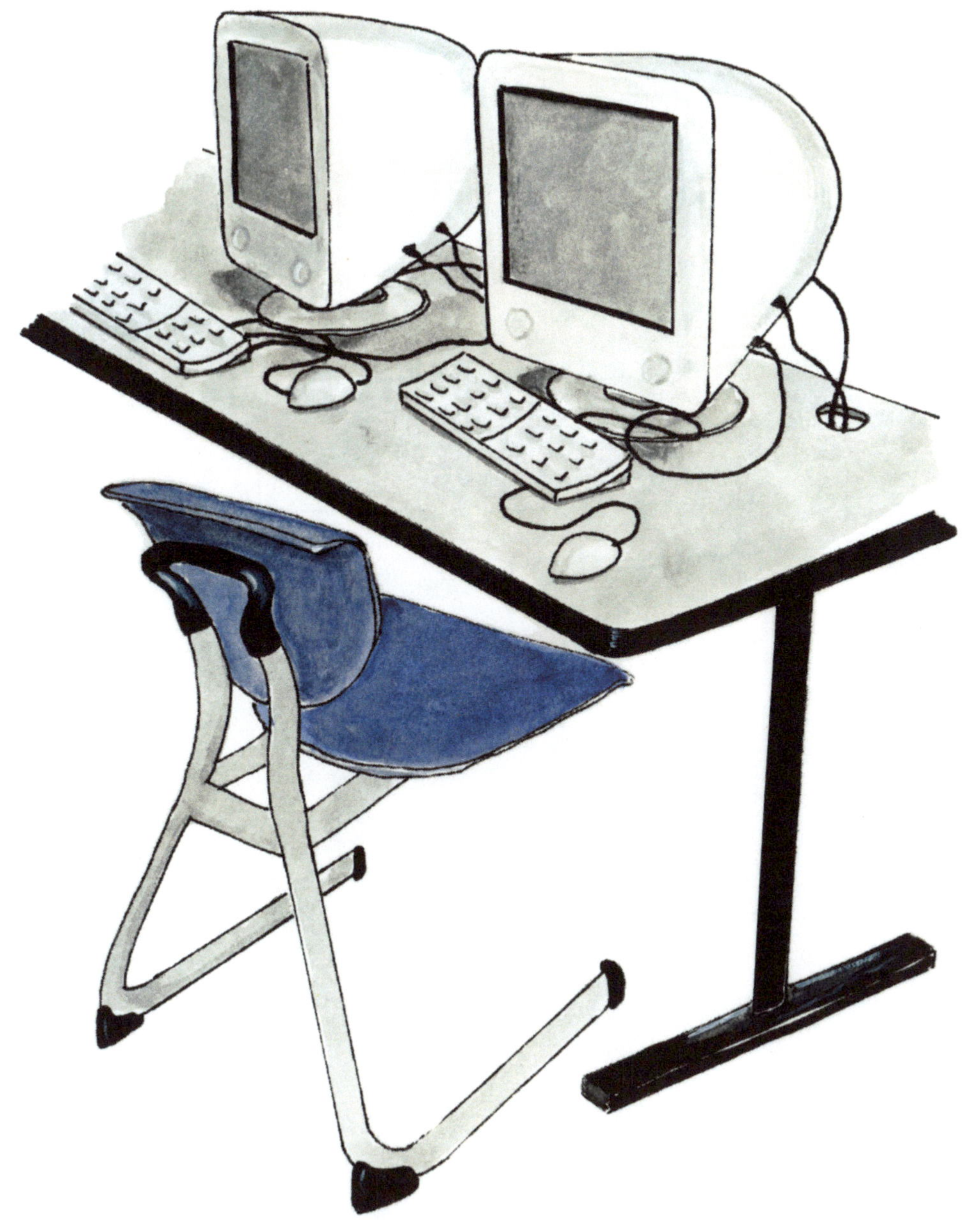

This was my favorite part of the day! We had computers for playing games, construction toys to build, housekeeping to play house, and a loft for reading.

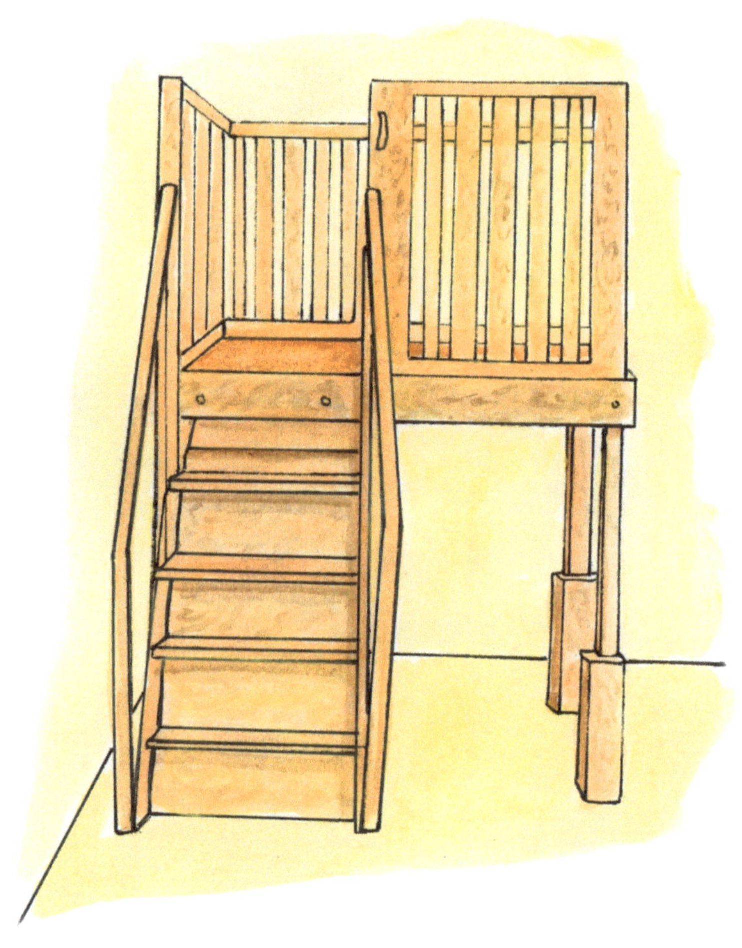

Sometimes I got to be the loft rester! I loved to sleep in the loft.

We went to the playground!

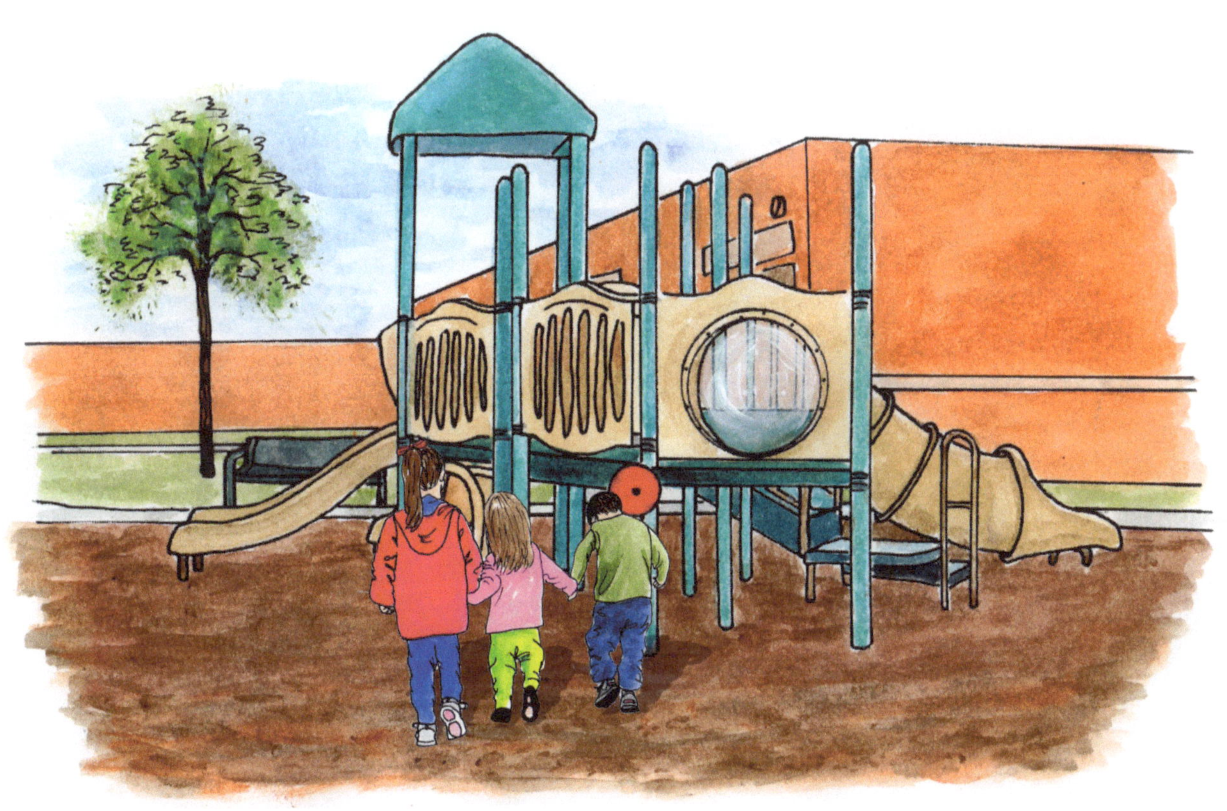

Recess is a part of kindergarten, too. Learning to play with your friends is important. Sometimes Mrs. Hookstra had to help us. She was always kind.

Look at our line.

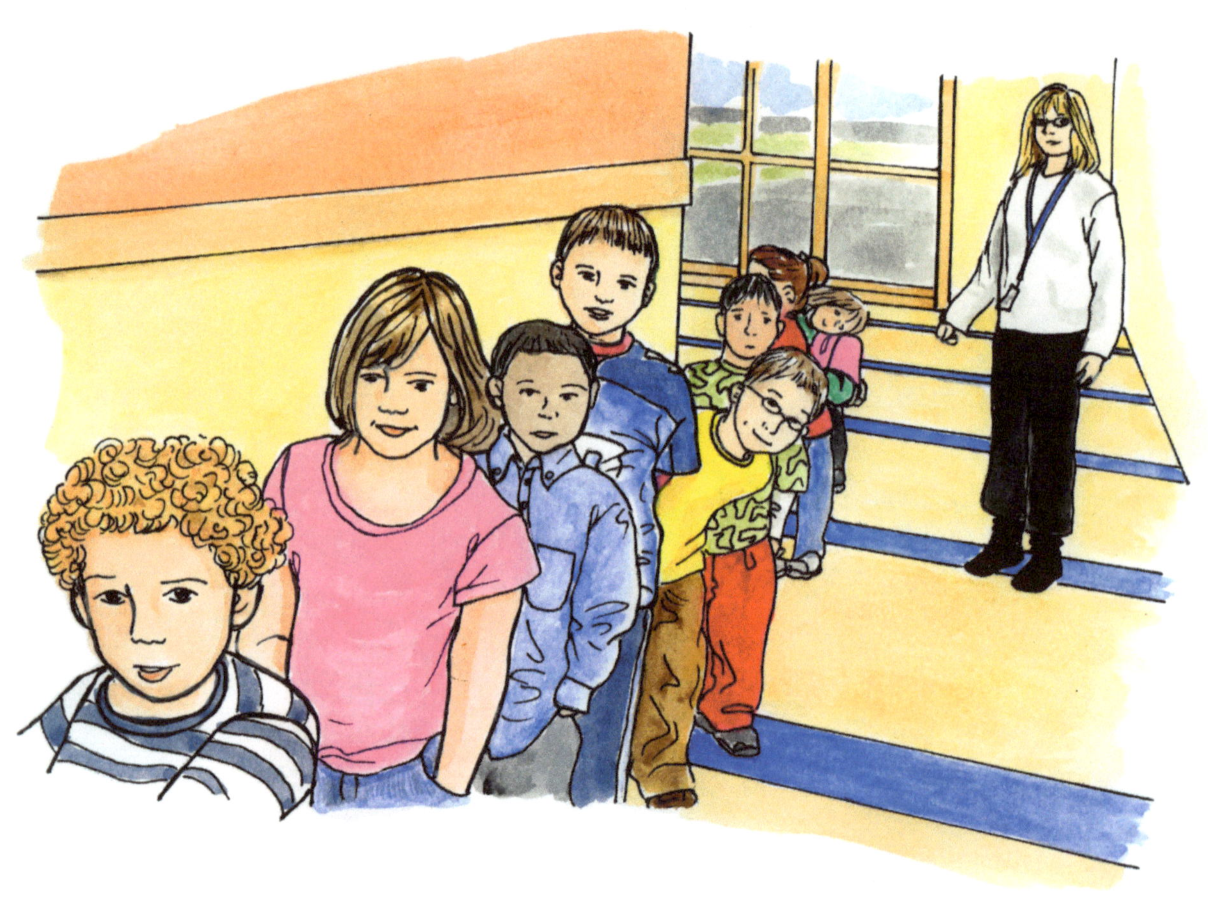

Walking in the hallway is important! It is not safe to run or hop in the halls, even though it is fun.

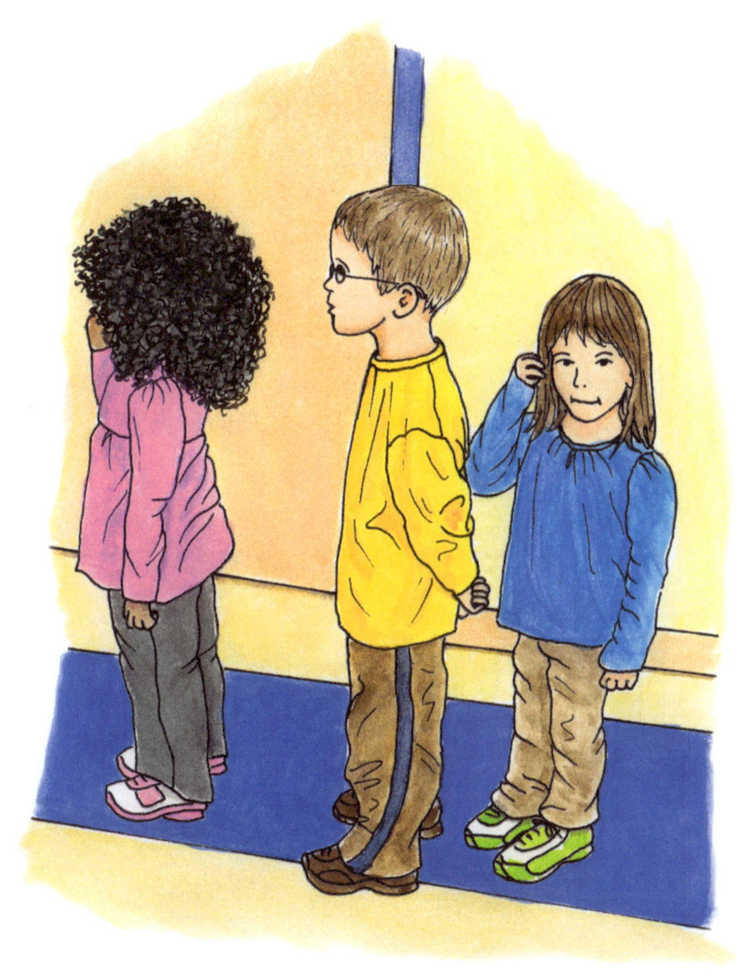

We also had to look forward, stay close (not too close) and to put a bubble in our mouth (not a real one). Our line took us to art, music, gym, library, and lunch!

Look at the animals.

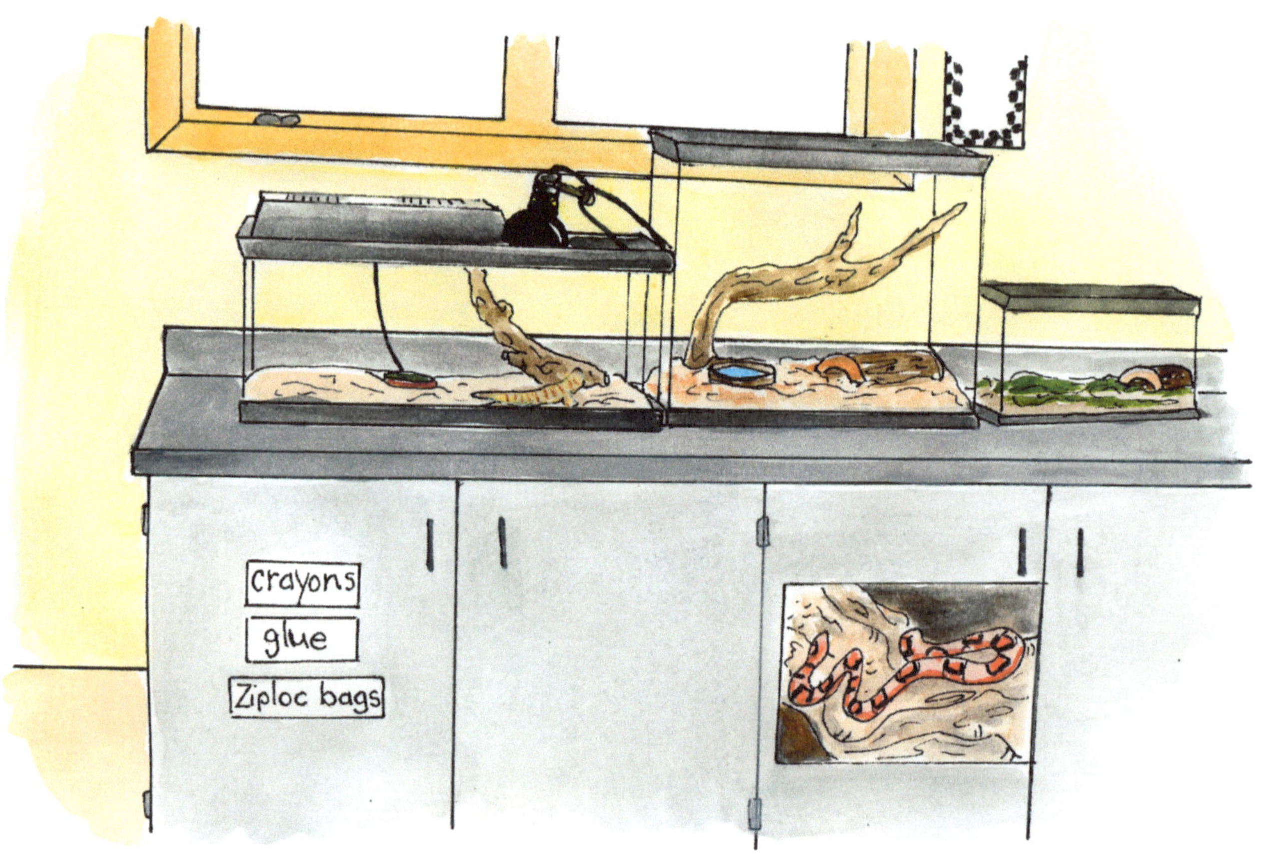

We had class pets. There was Spike, the bearded dragon, and Kermit, a tree frog. Learning to love the animals helped us to not be afraid of them. Like the animals, my classmates needed to be respected, too! Mrs. Hookstra taught us how to show respect.

See the snake?

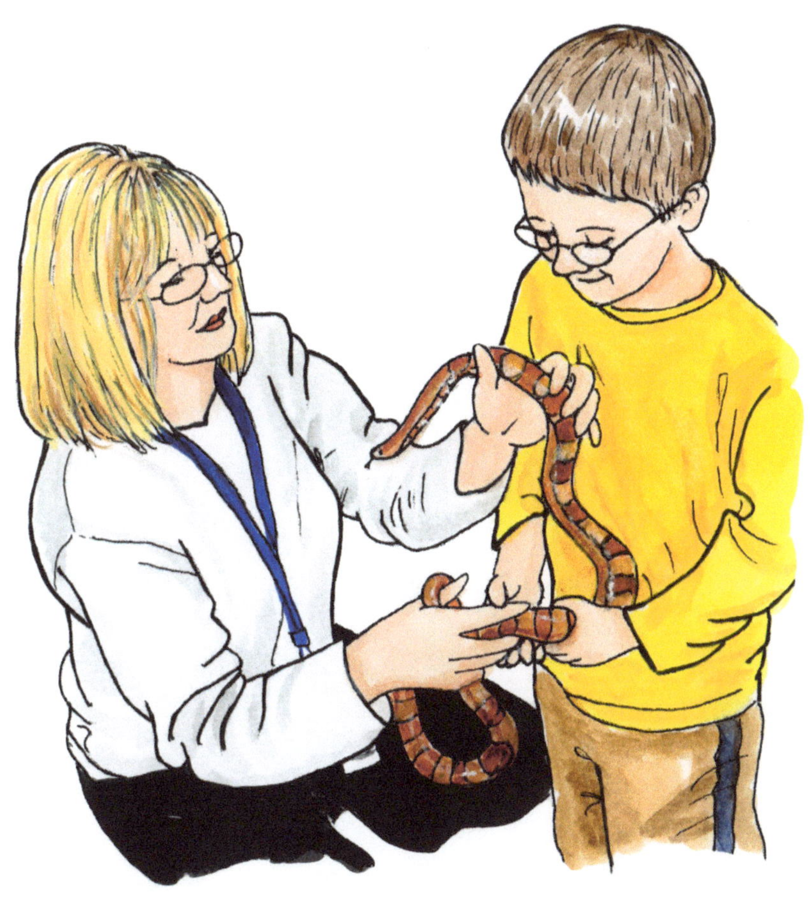

Popcorn was a snake. We got to hold it! We always washed our hands after holding the animals. It was important to stay healthy. No one wanted to miss school!

Here is my friend.

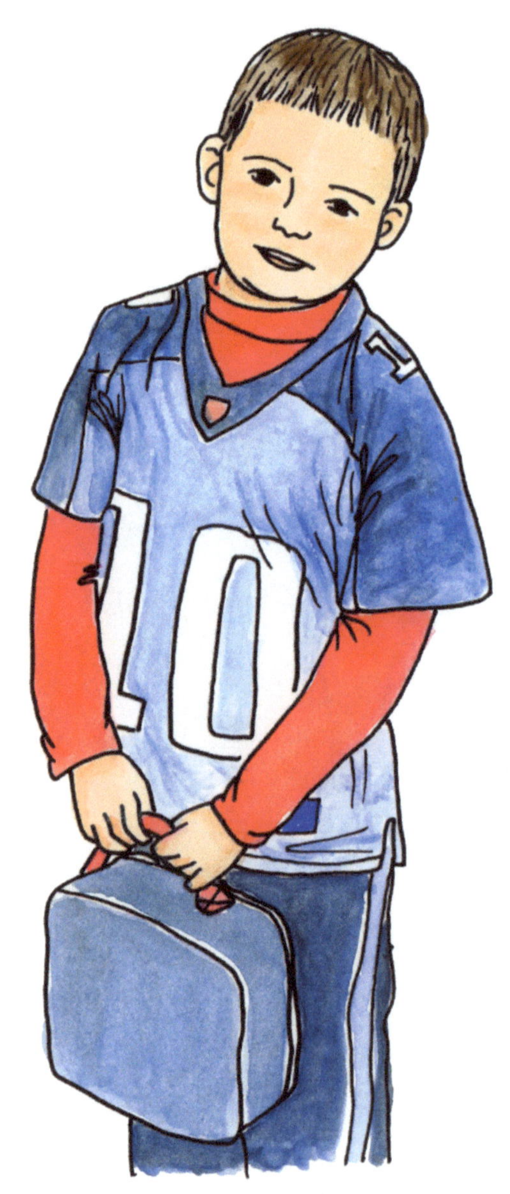

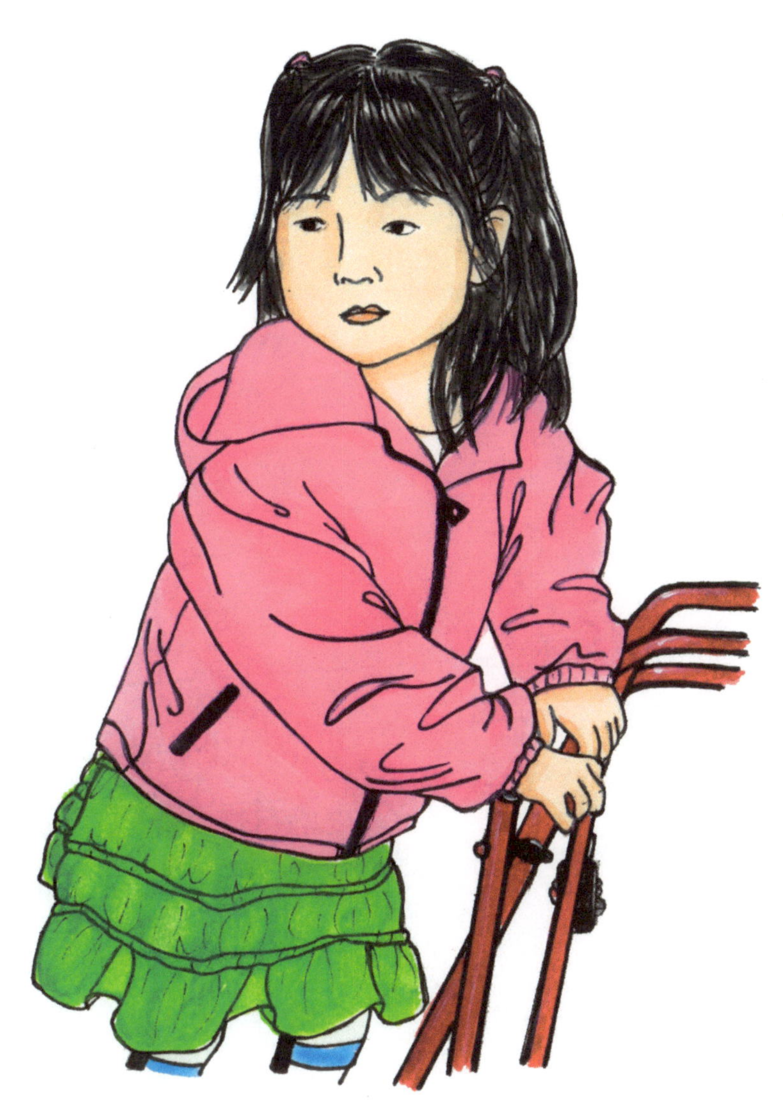

I made so many friends. One friend got very sick and couldn't come to school. We made her cards. Mrs. Hookstra taught us to be kind and caring. I learned that it made others feel good, and it made me feel really good inside, too! We were glad when she got better and came back.

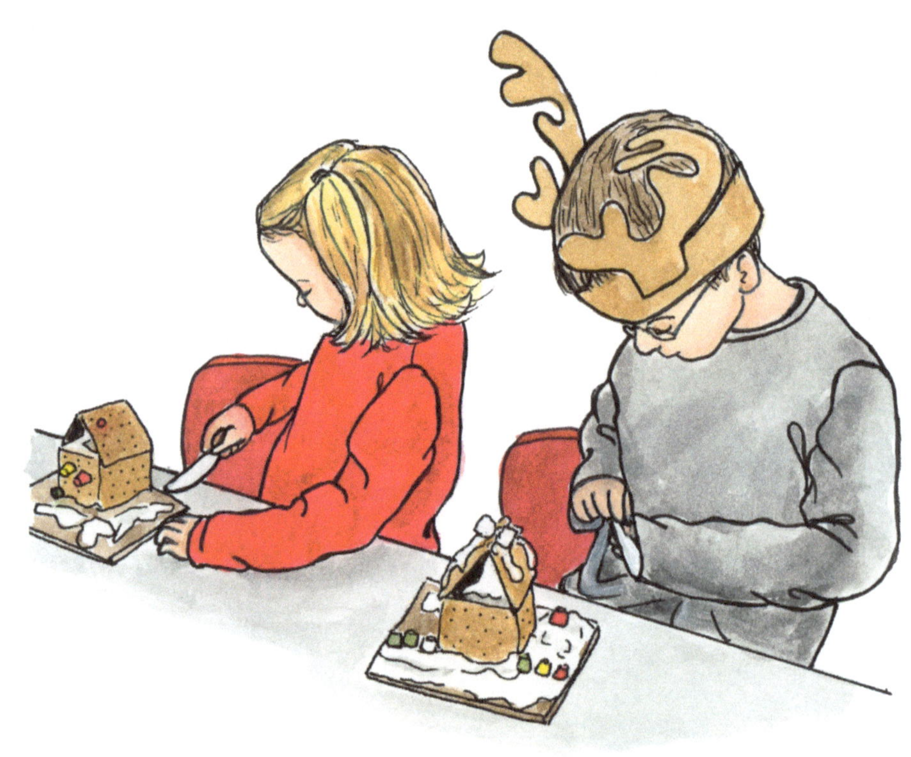

During the holidays, we made gingerbread houses, reindeer antlers and
Native American vests.

Look at our hats.

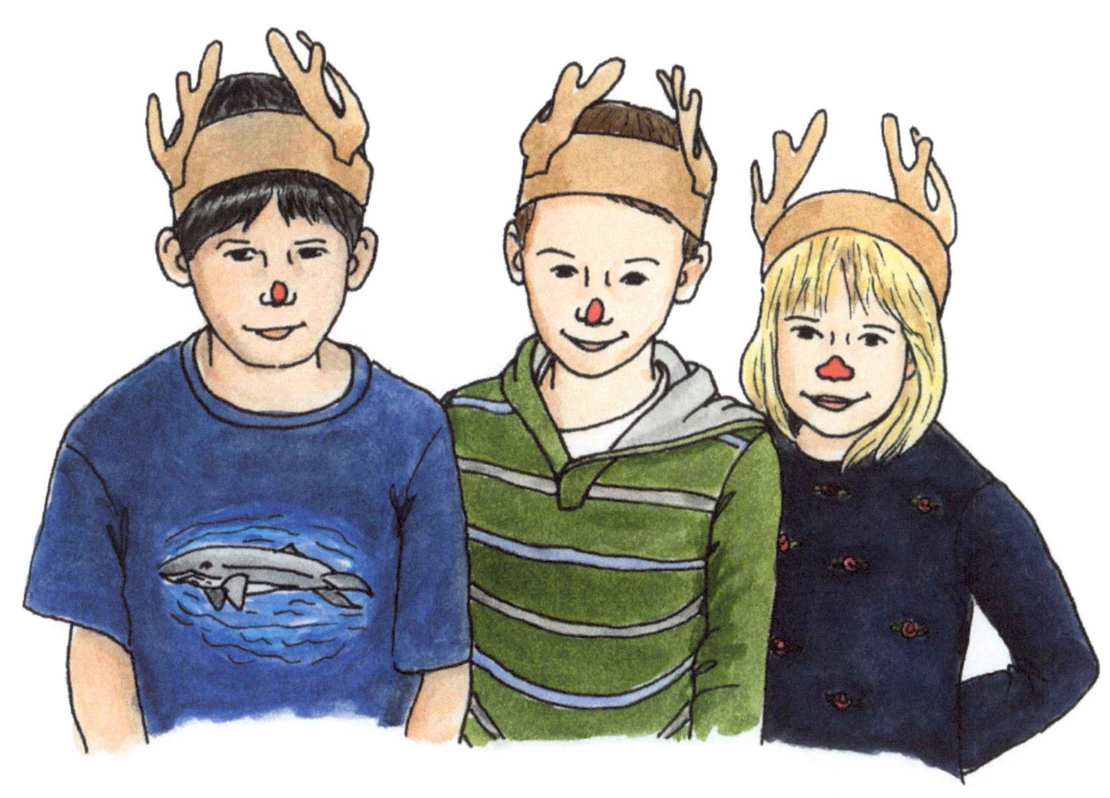

We sang special songs. We traveled the world and brought the rainforest back to our classroom. No one believed us, so we showed the whole school.

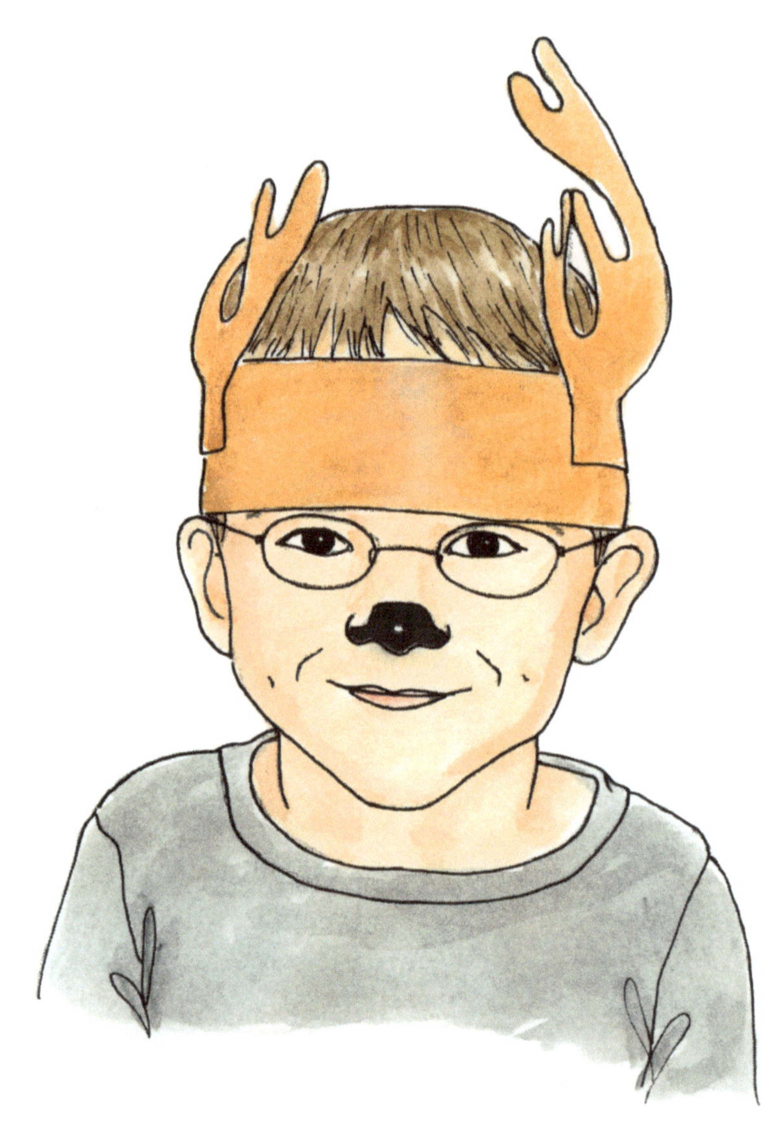

Mrs. Hookstra planned fun things everyday!

Here is my mom and dad.

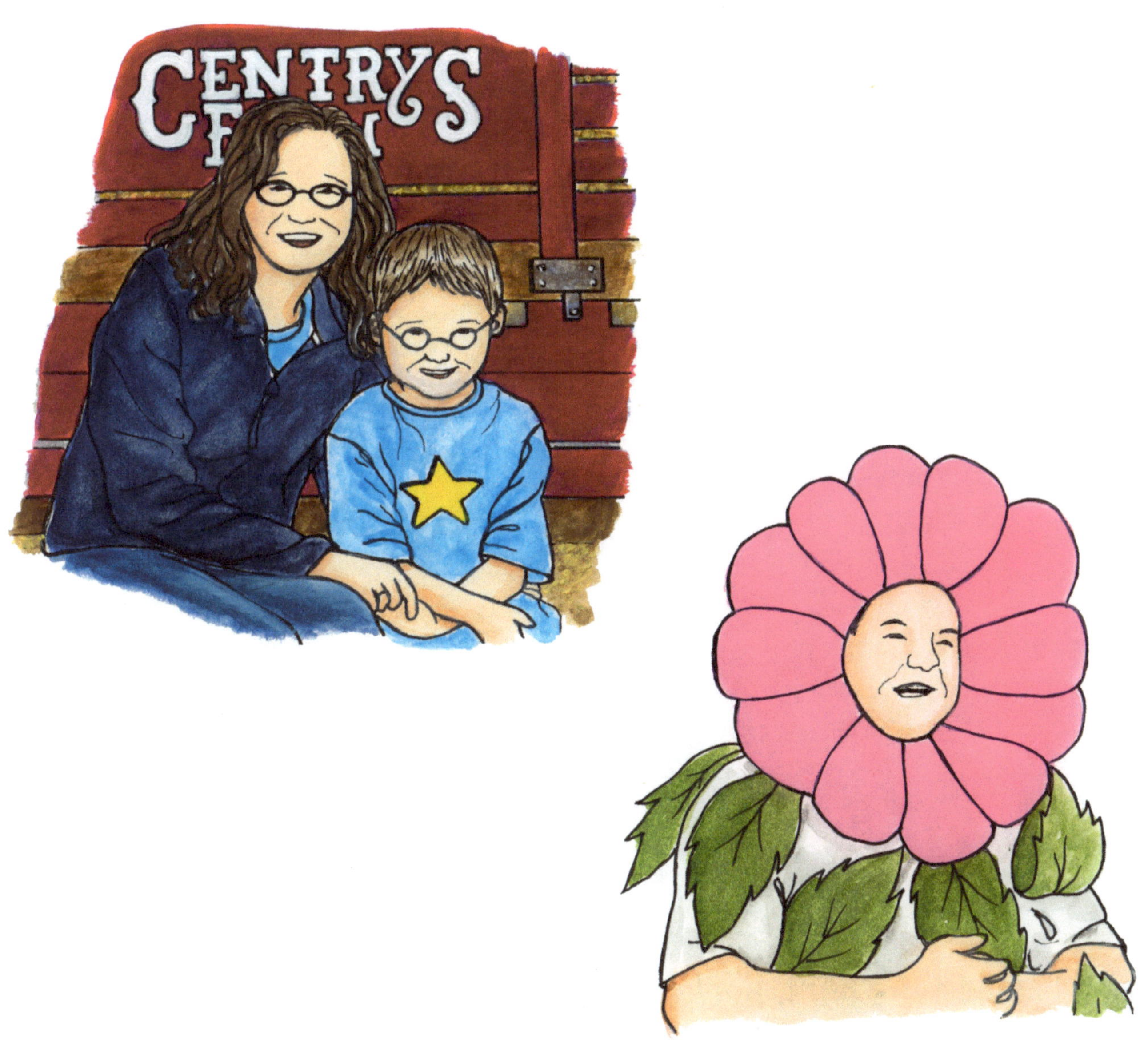

Our class went on field trips and had special projects. Sometimes my mom and dad got to help. I learned that parents of kindergarteners really like to do that! It was fun going places.

Look at me. I am going to first grade.

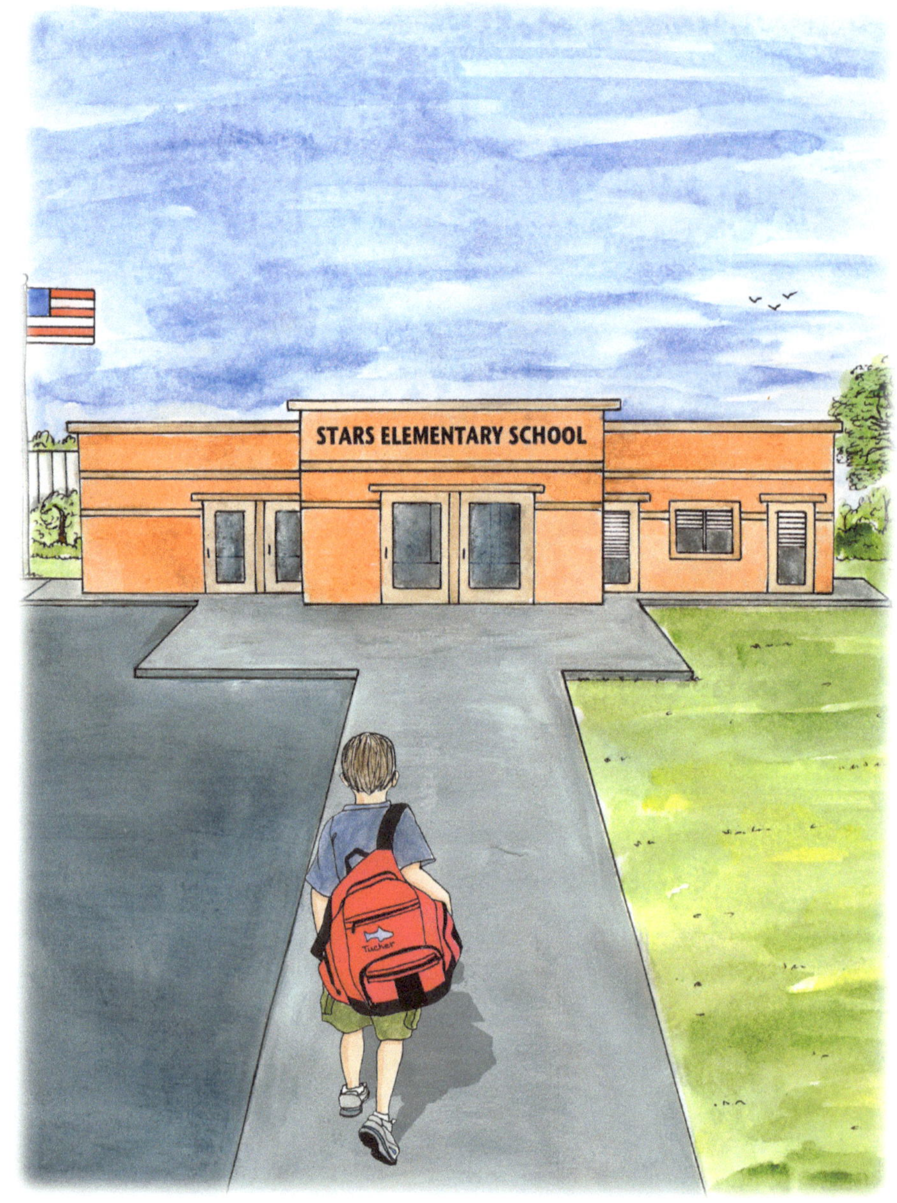

I wish I could take Mrs. Hookstra to first grade with me. But I can't because other kindergarten students need her, just like I did. On second thought, I guess I am taking a little bit of her with me. I will always know how to move in the halls, be ready for school, read, and be nice to my friends. I know I am special, and I can make others feel special. If I need her, I will always know where to find her. She will be standing at her door every morning, hugging children, including me!

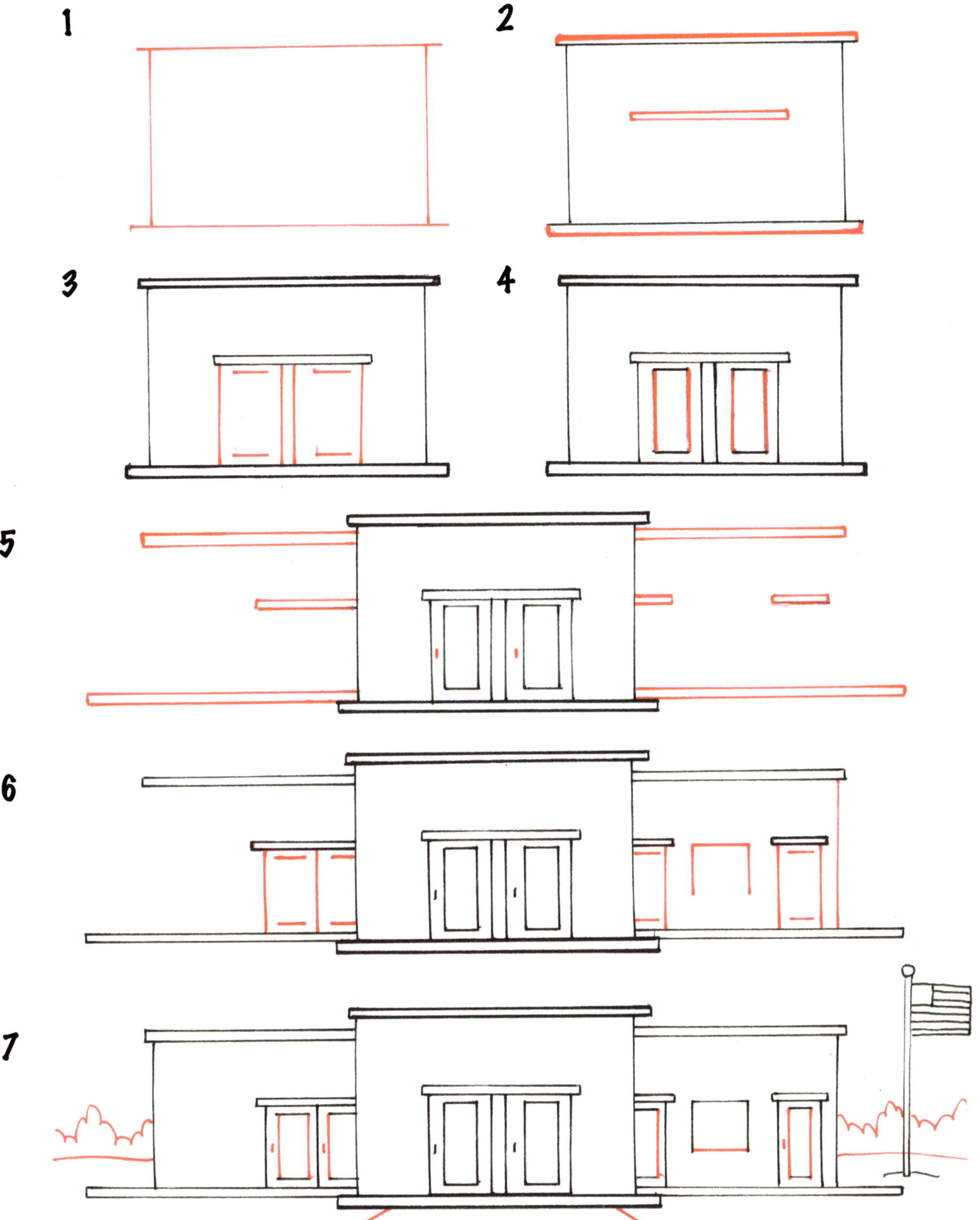

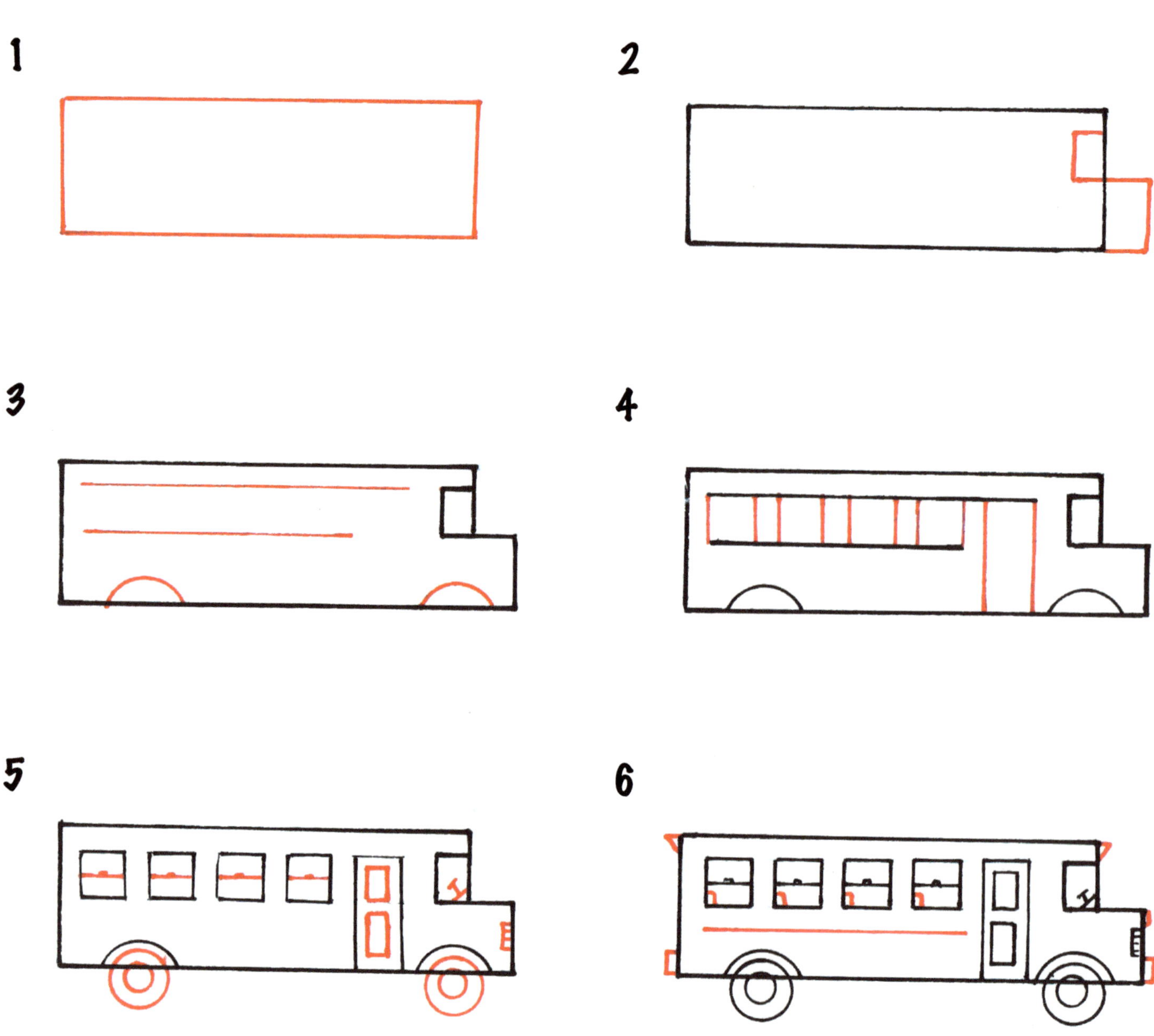

27

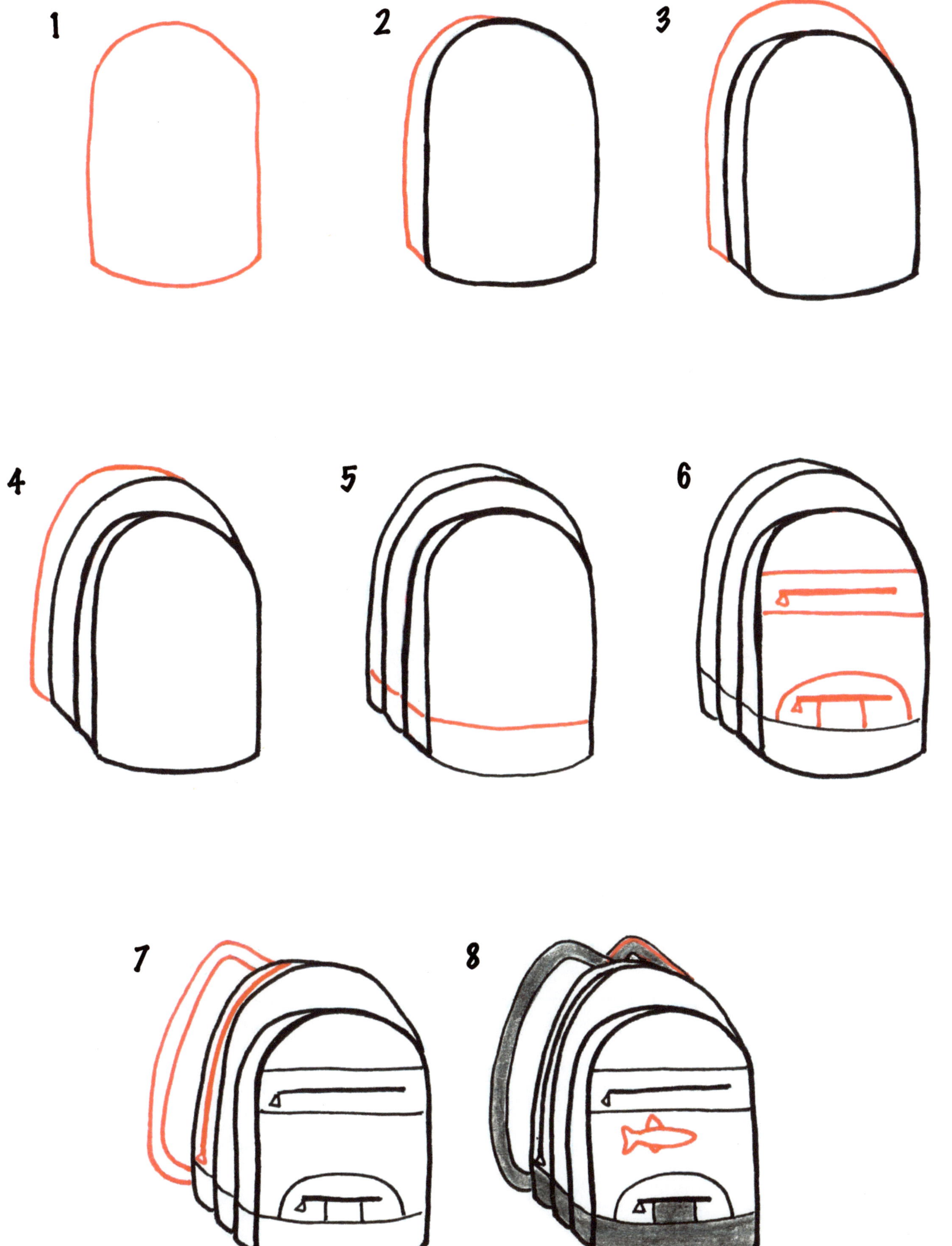

1
2
3
4
5
6
7
8

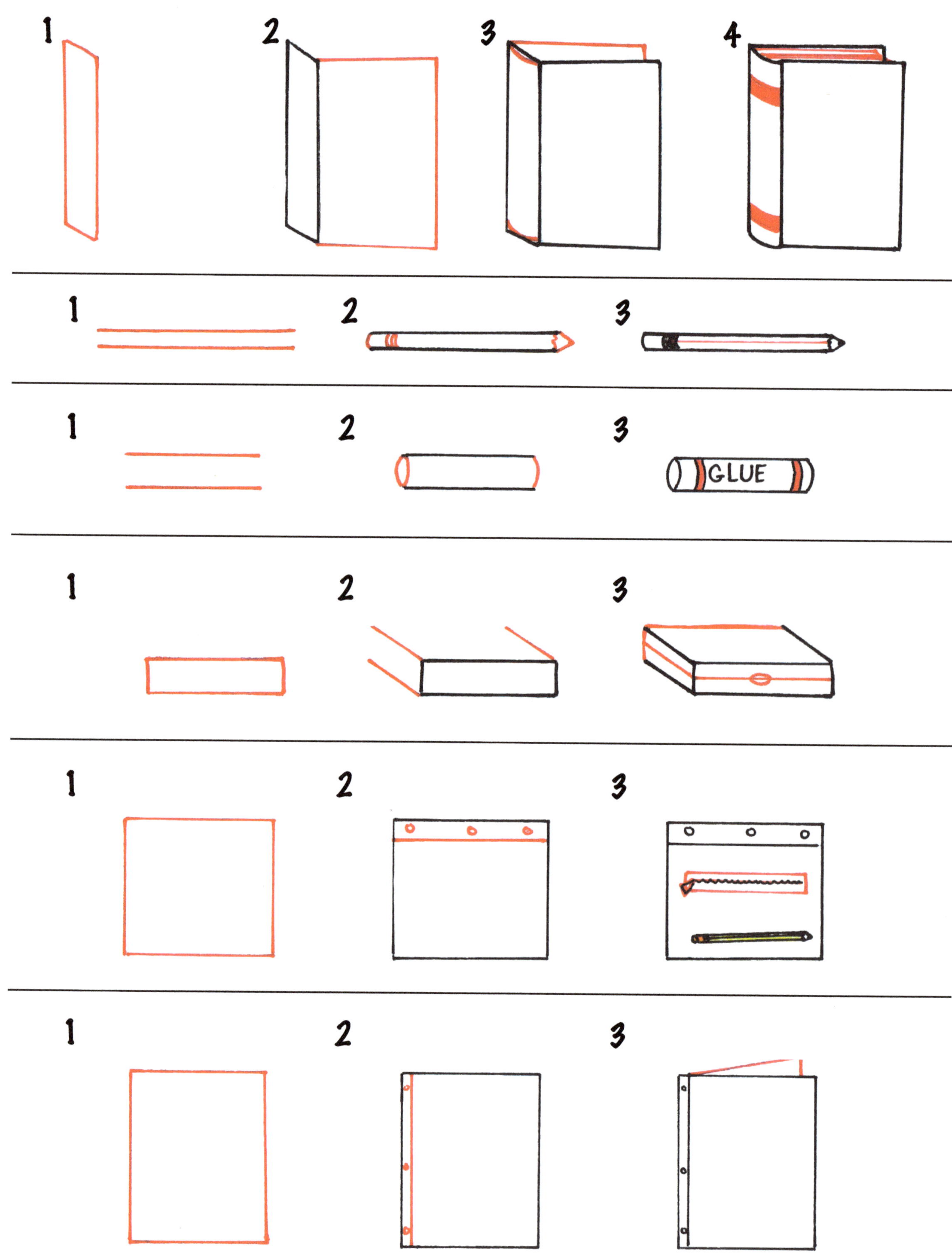
GLUE

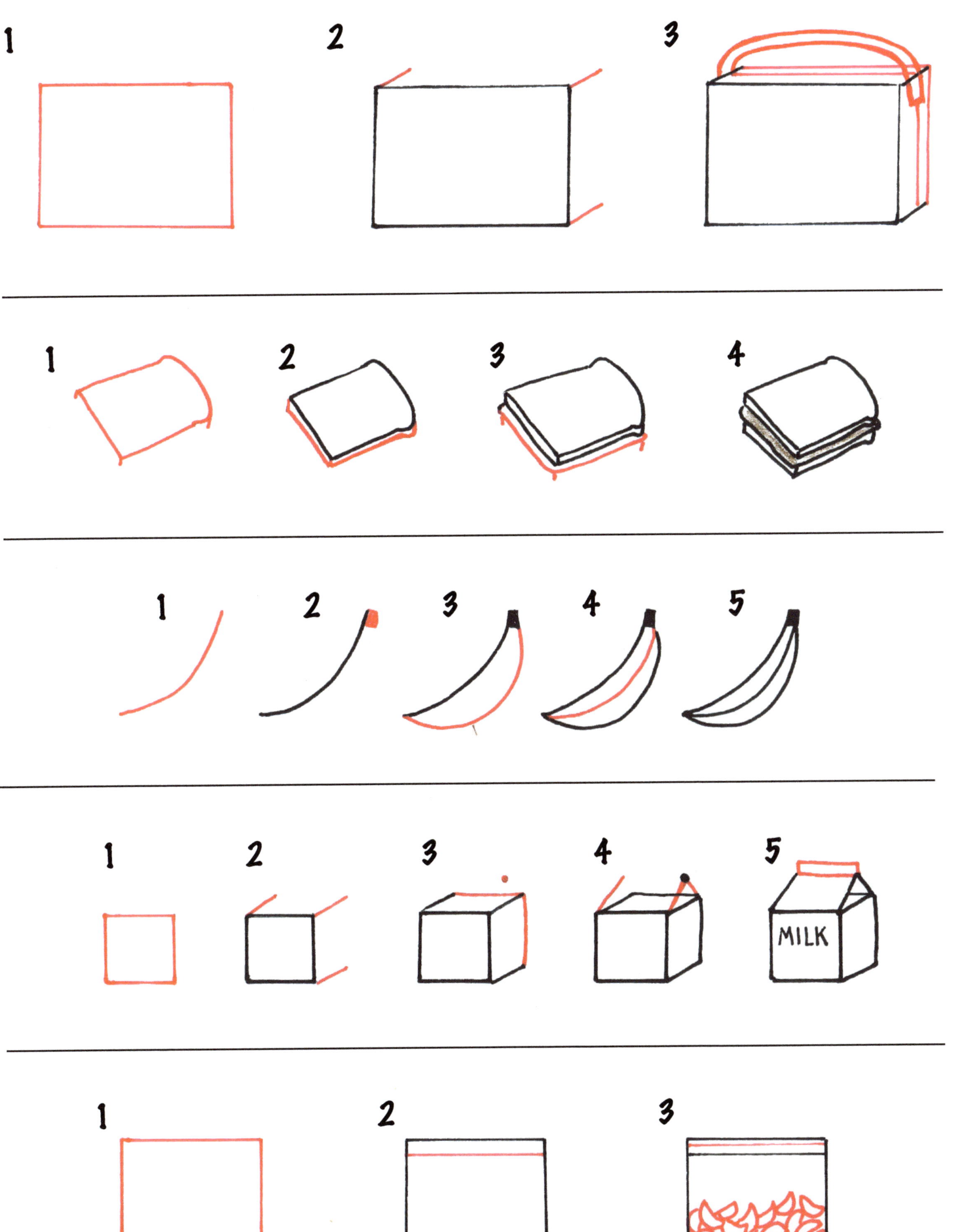
MILK

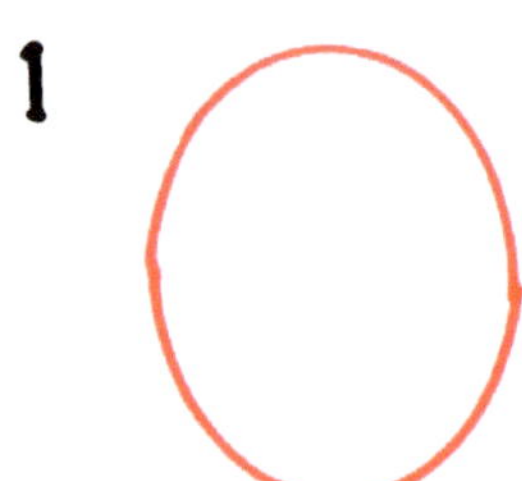

1

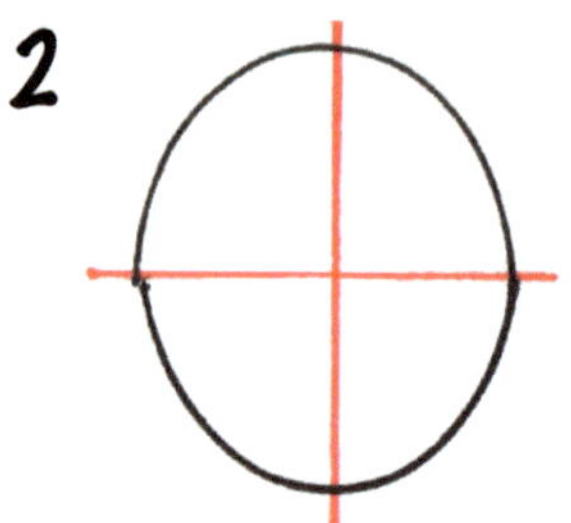

2

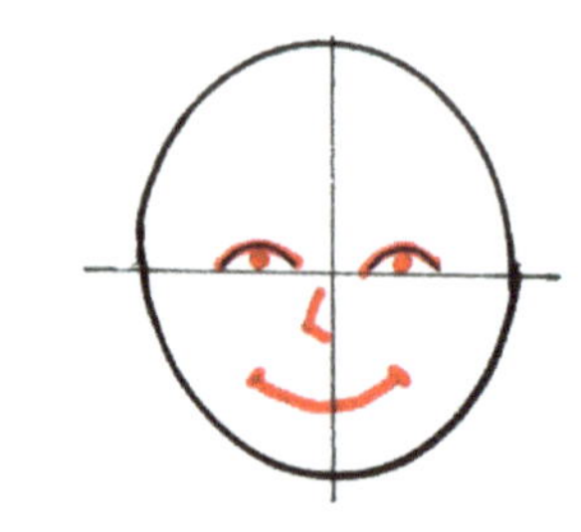

3

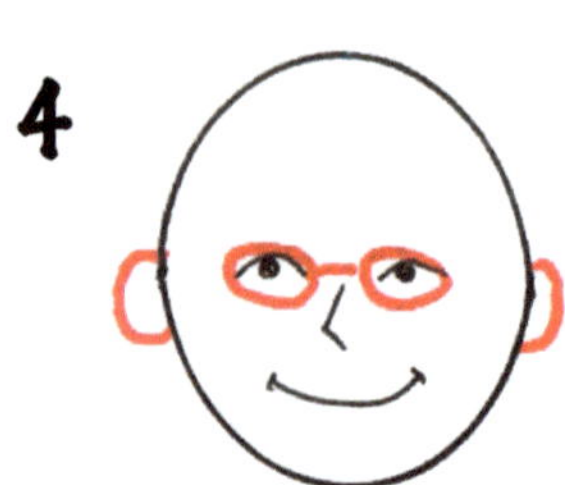

4

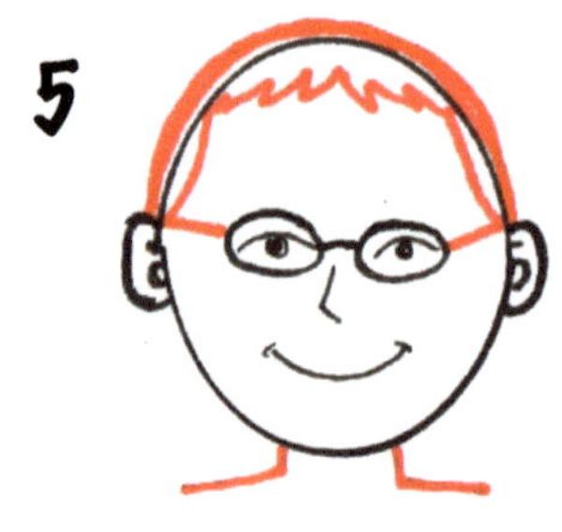

5

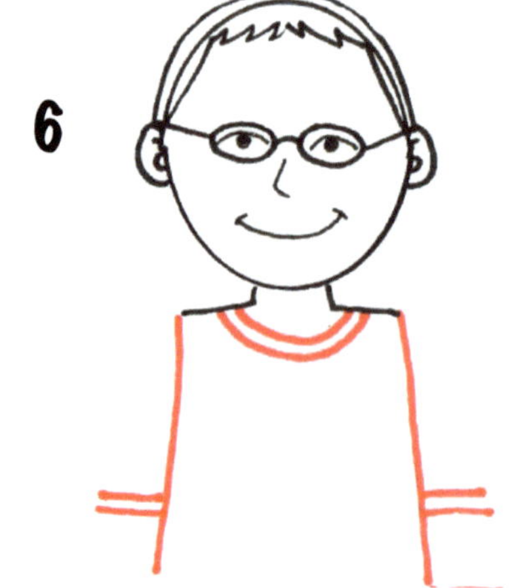

6

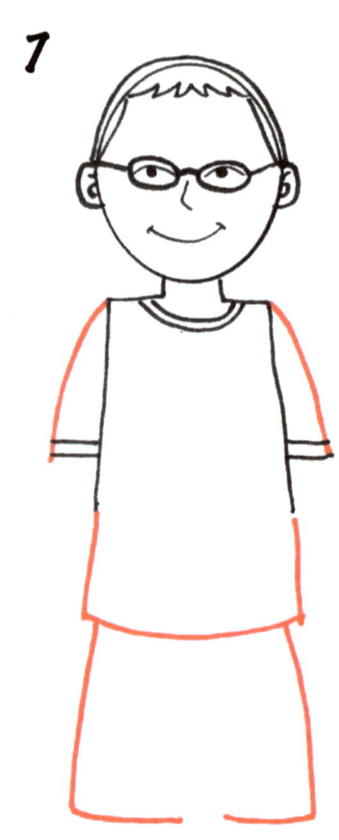

7

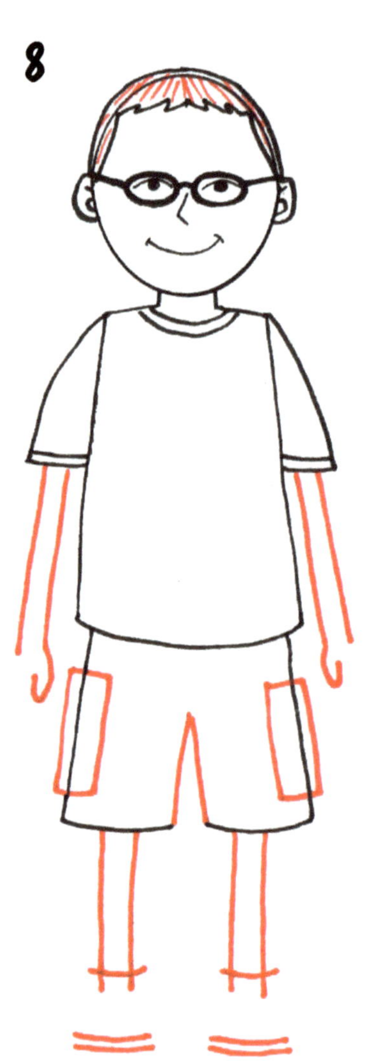

8

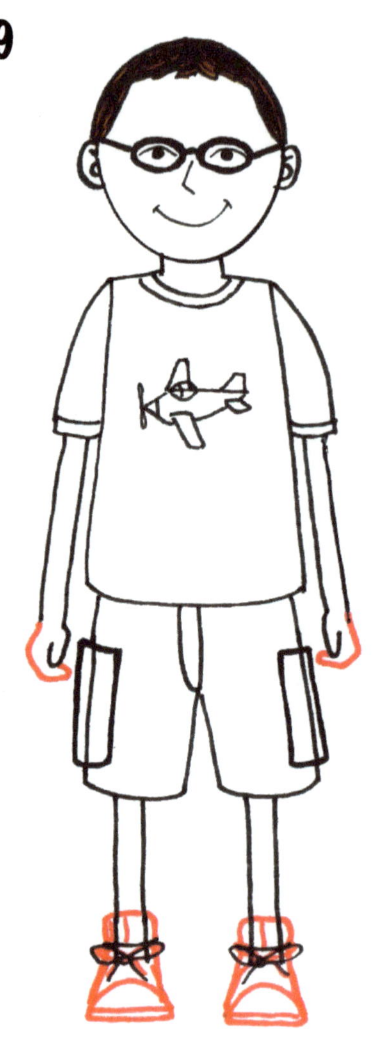

9

1

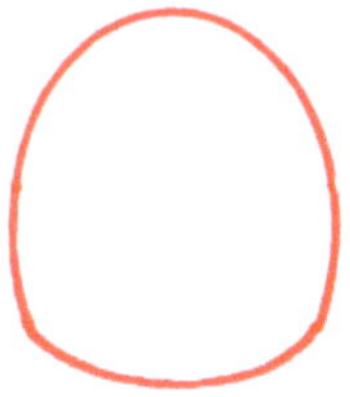

2

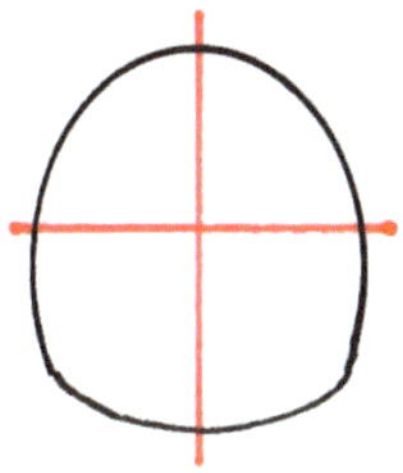

3

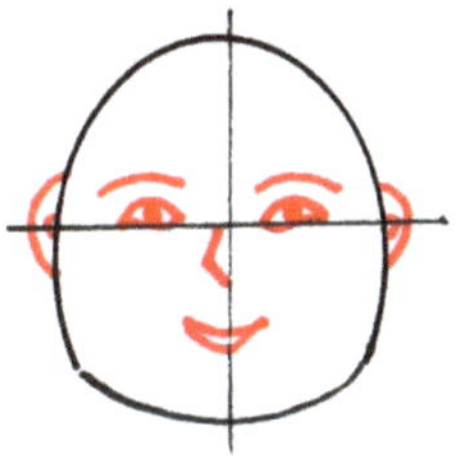

4

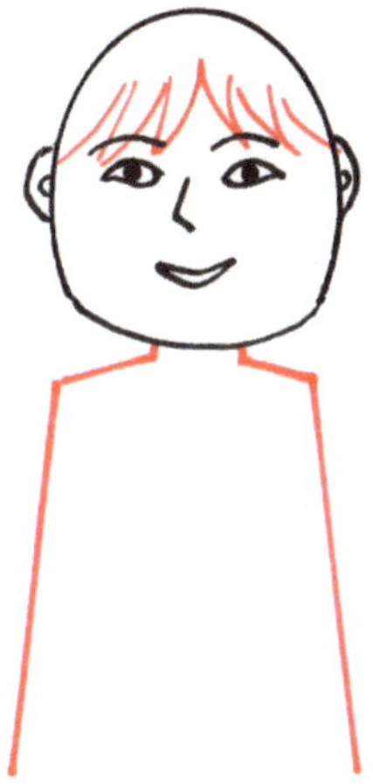

5

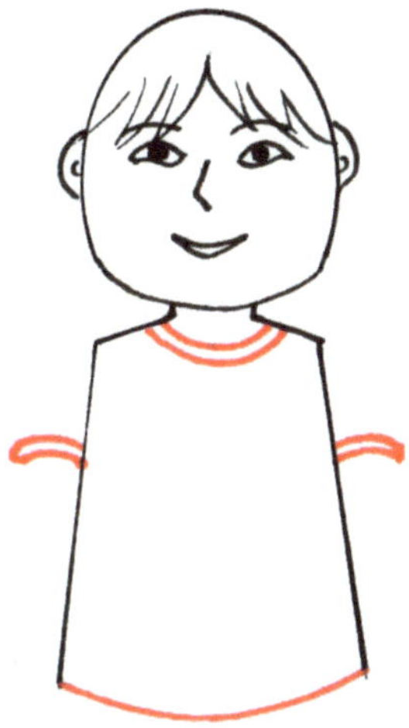

6

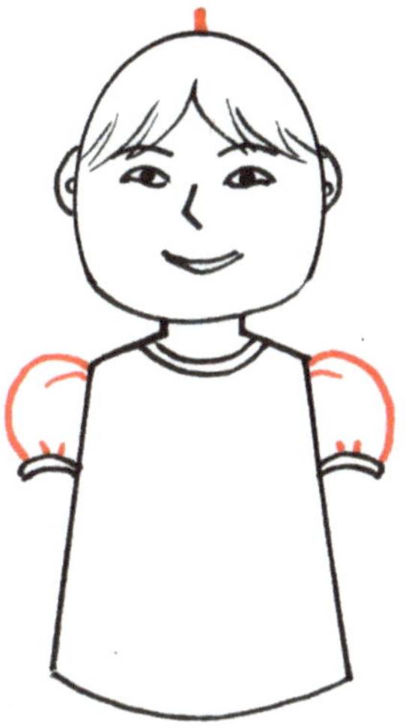

7

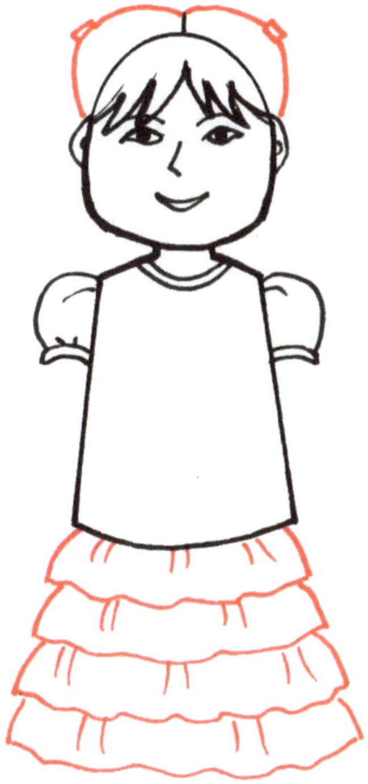

8

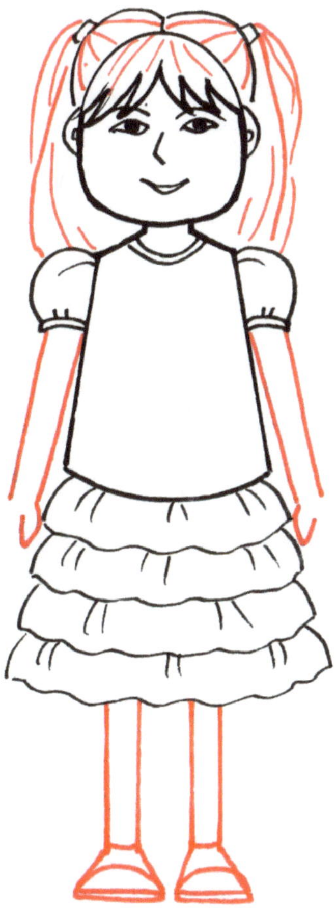

9

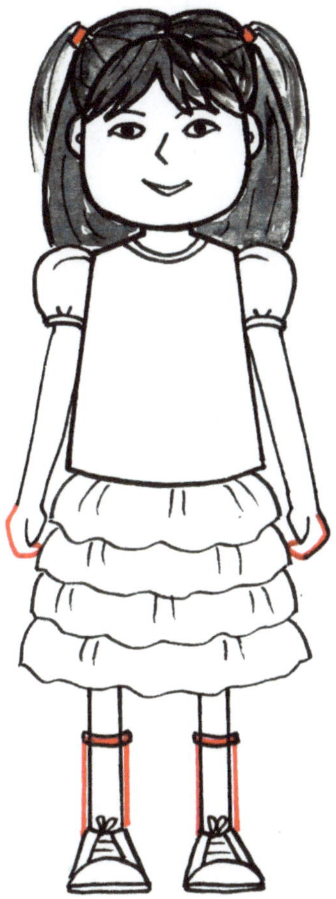

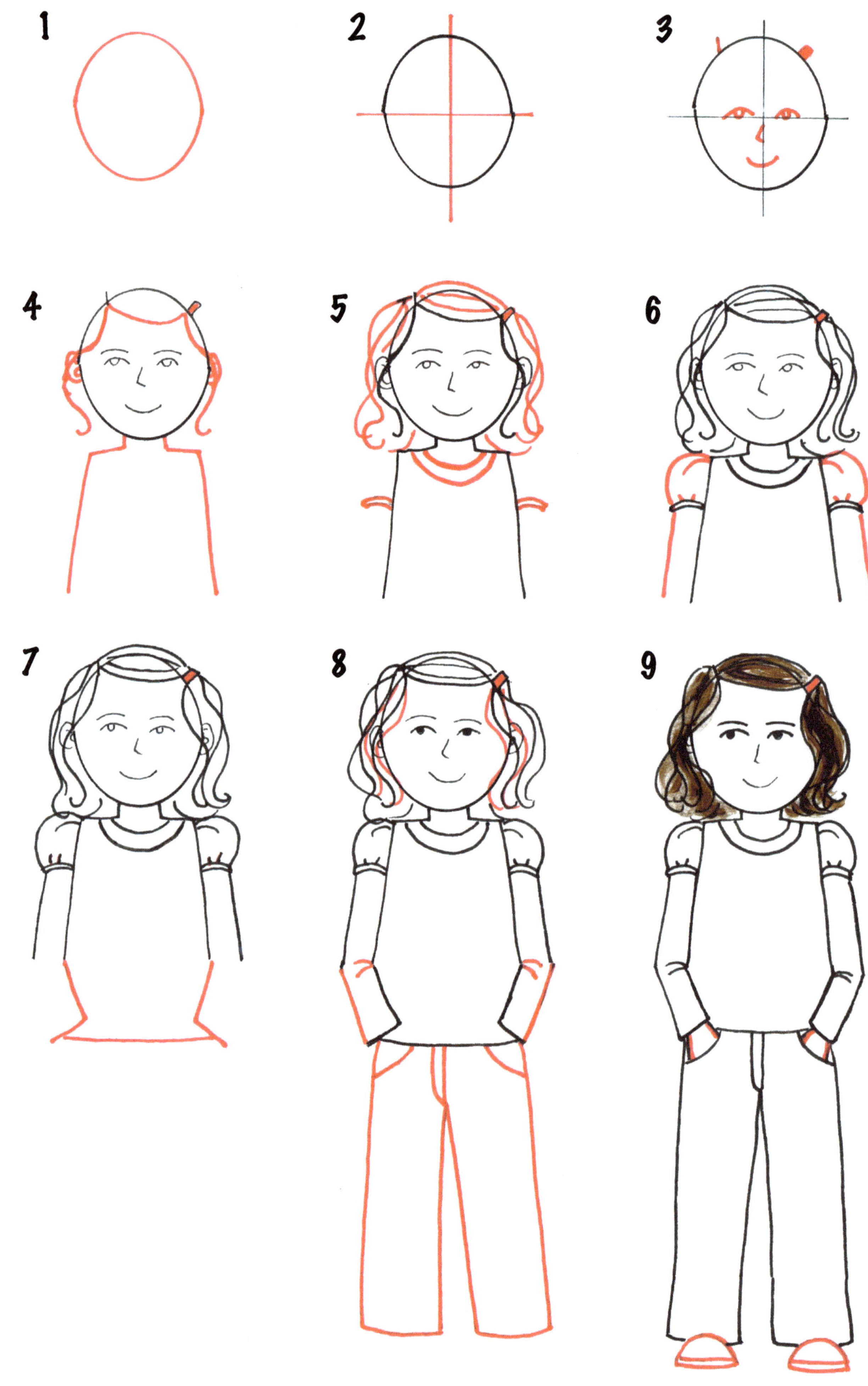

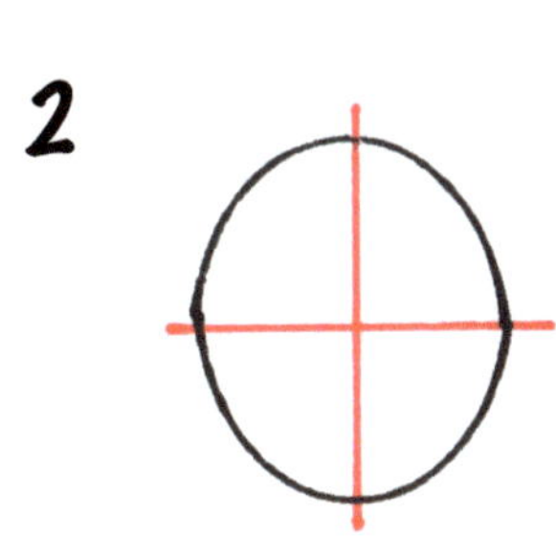

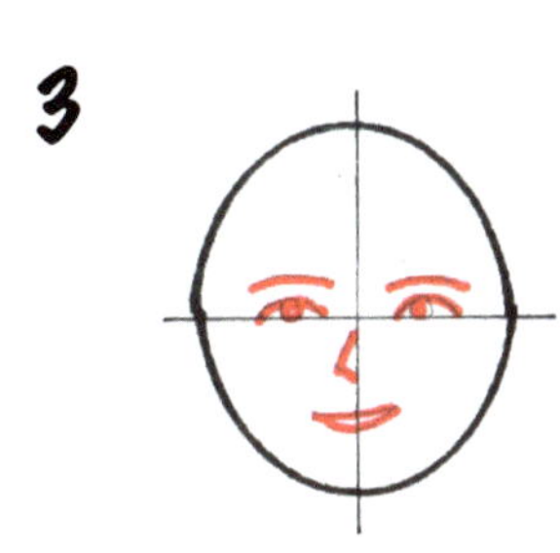

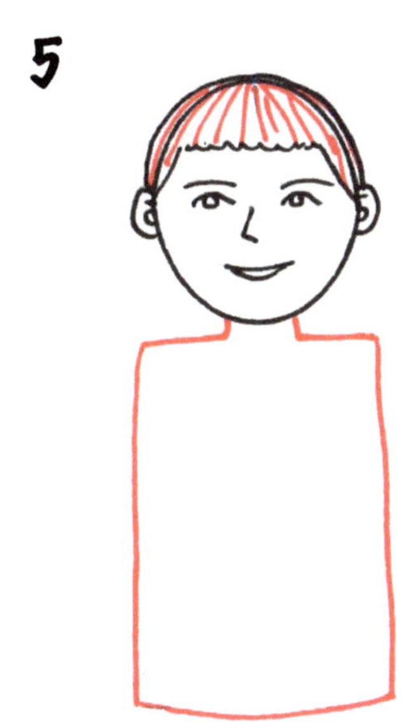

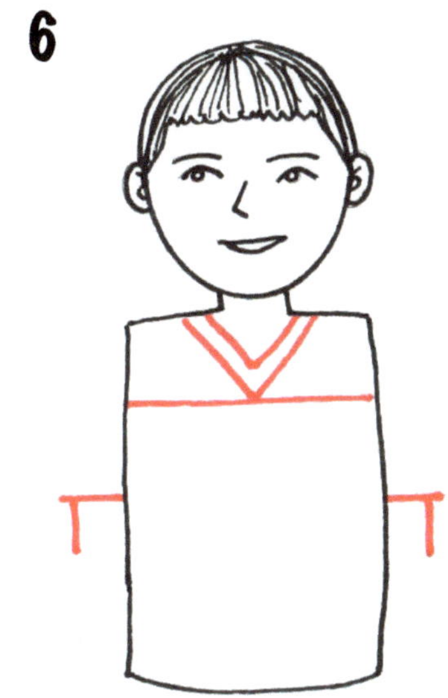

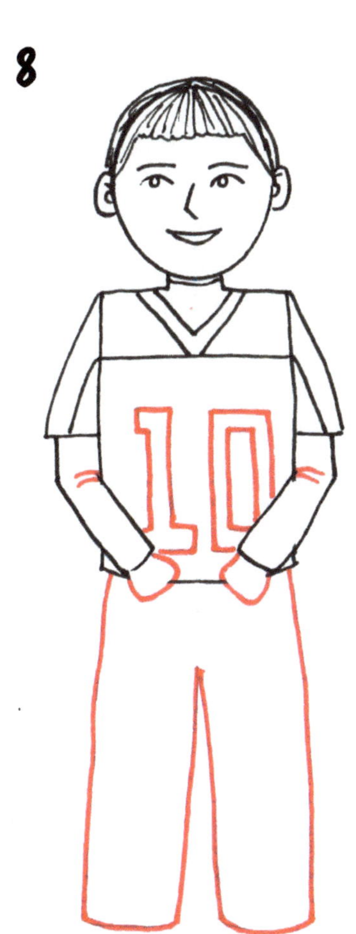

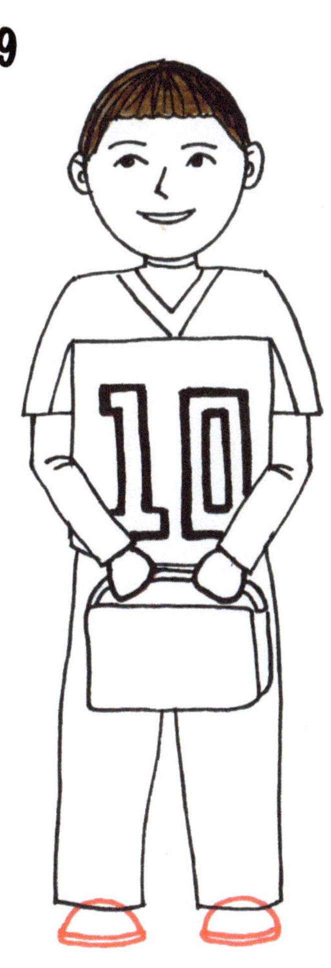

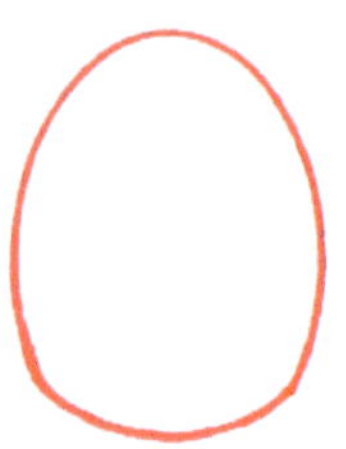

1

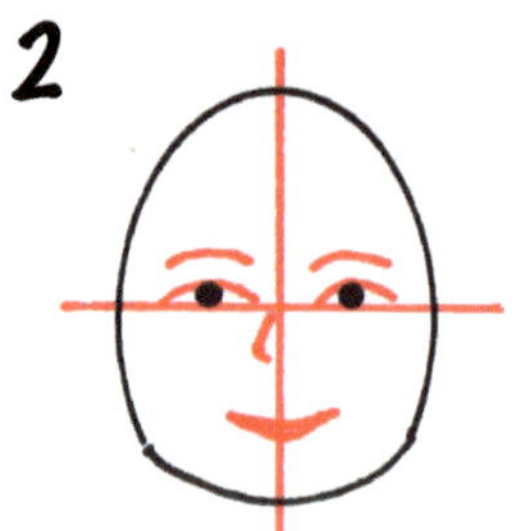

2

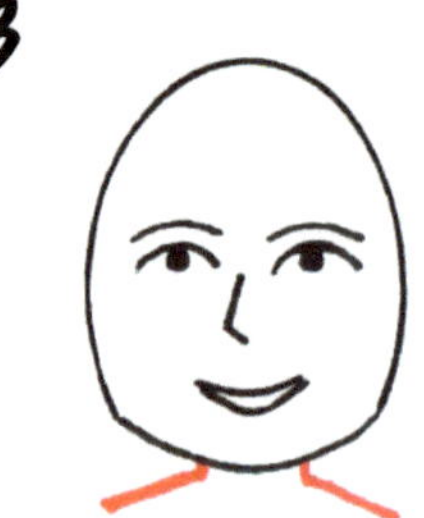

3

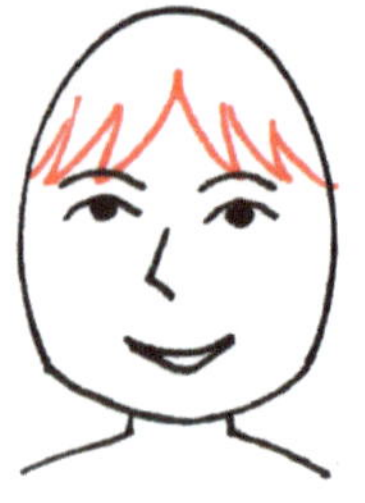

4

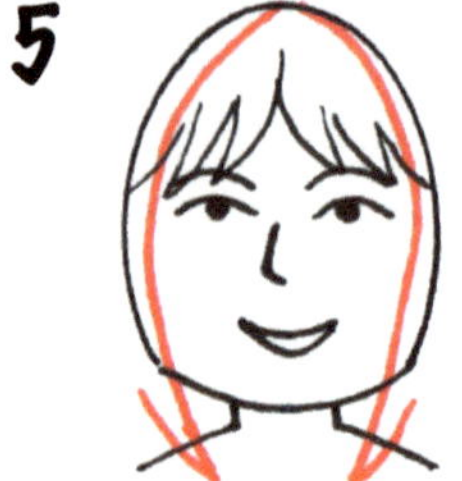

5

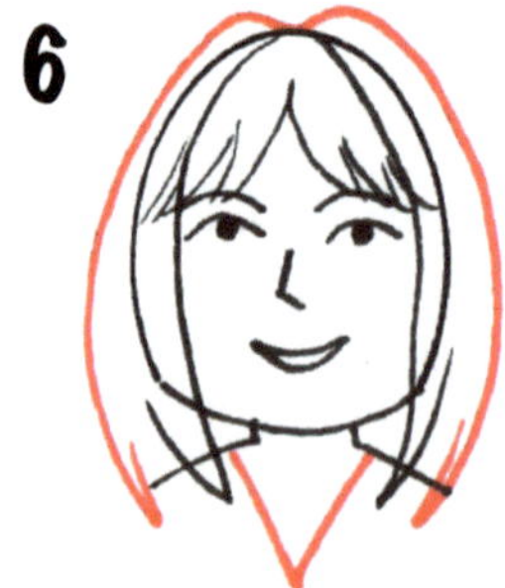

6

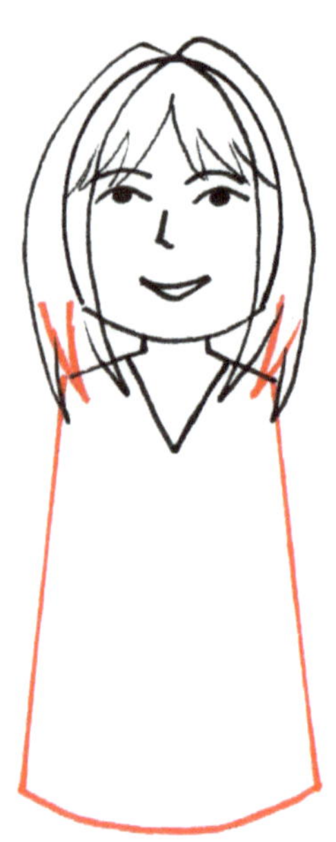

7

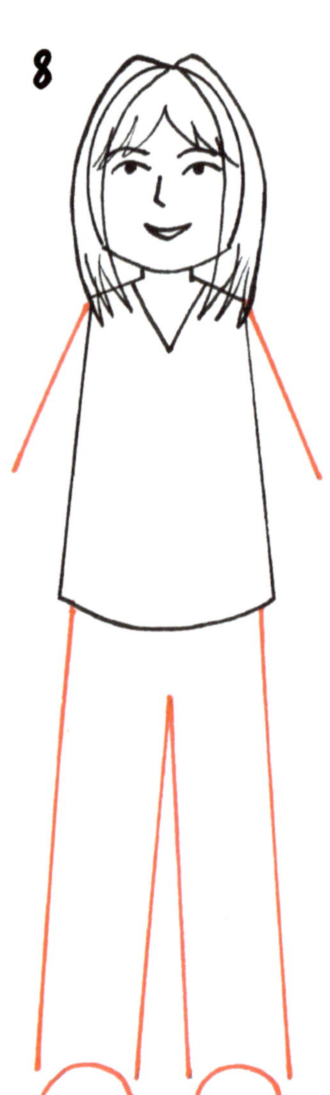

8

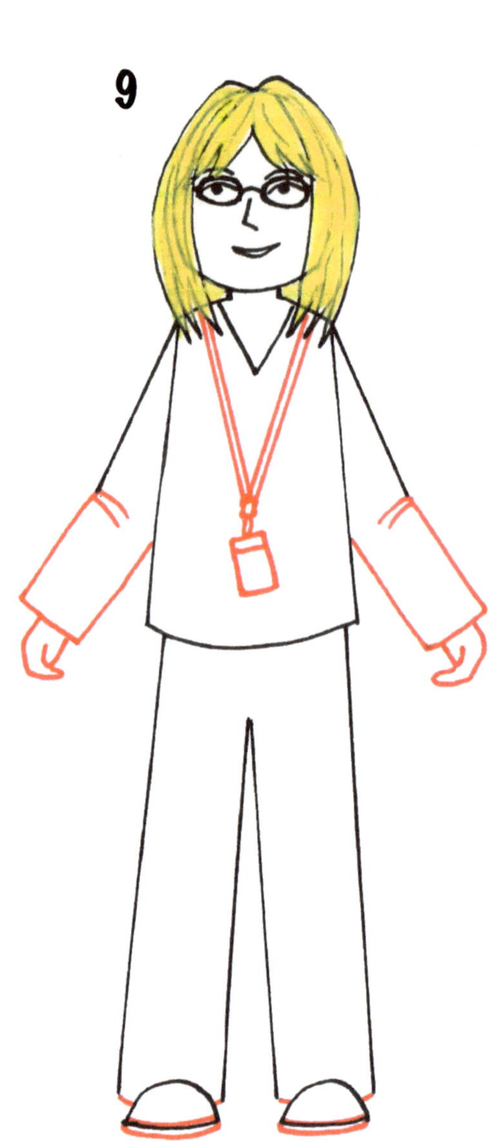

9

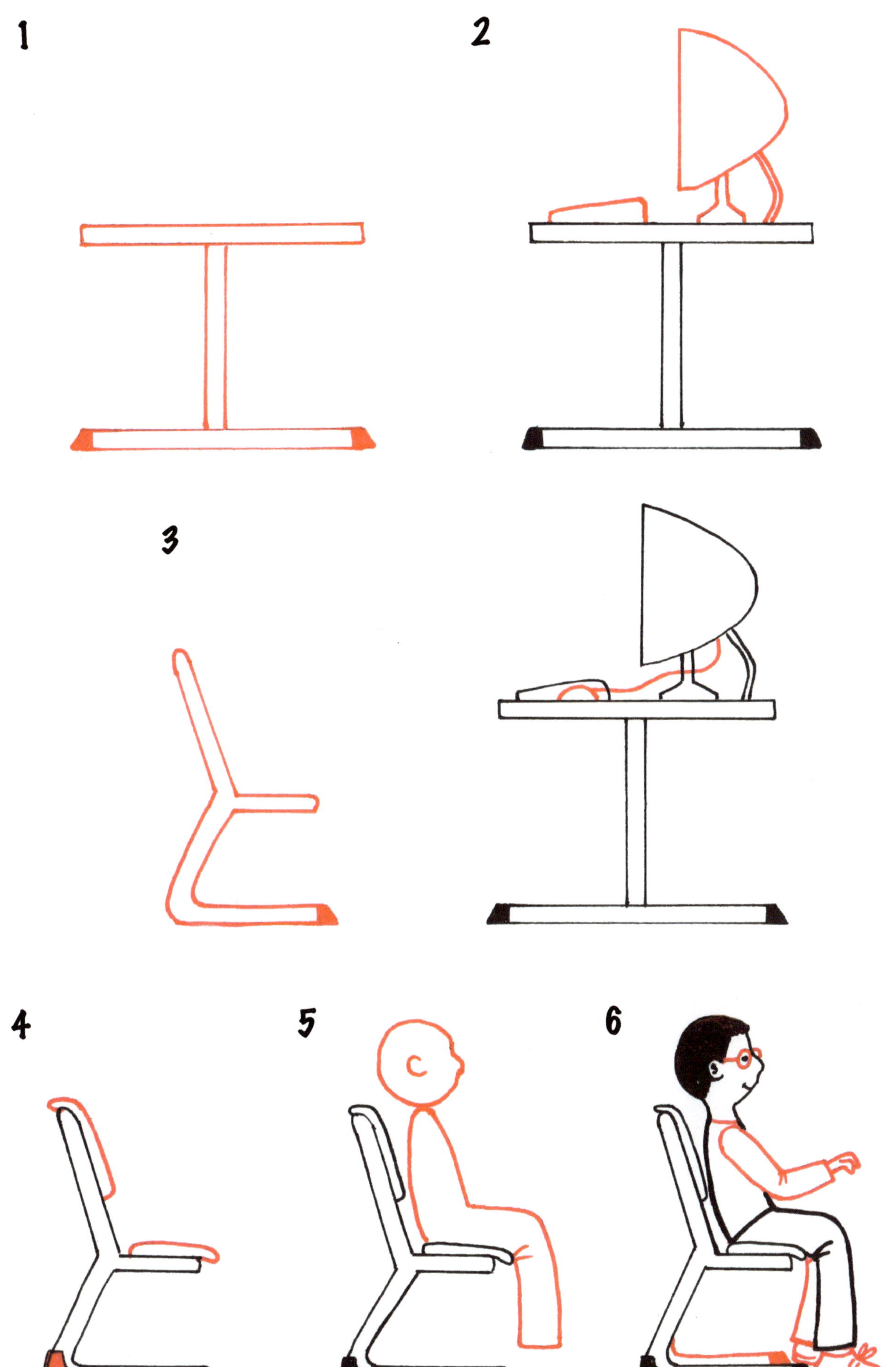

1
2
3
4
5
6

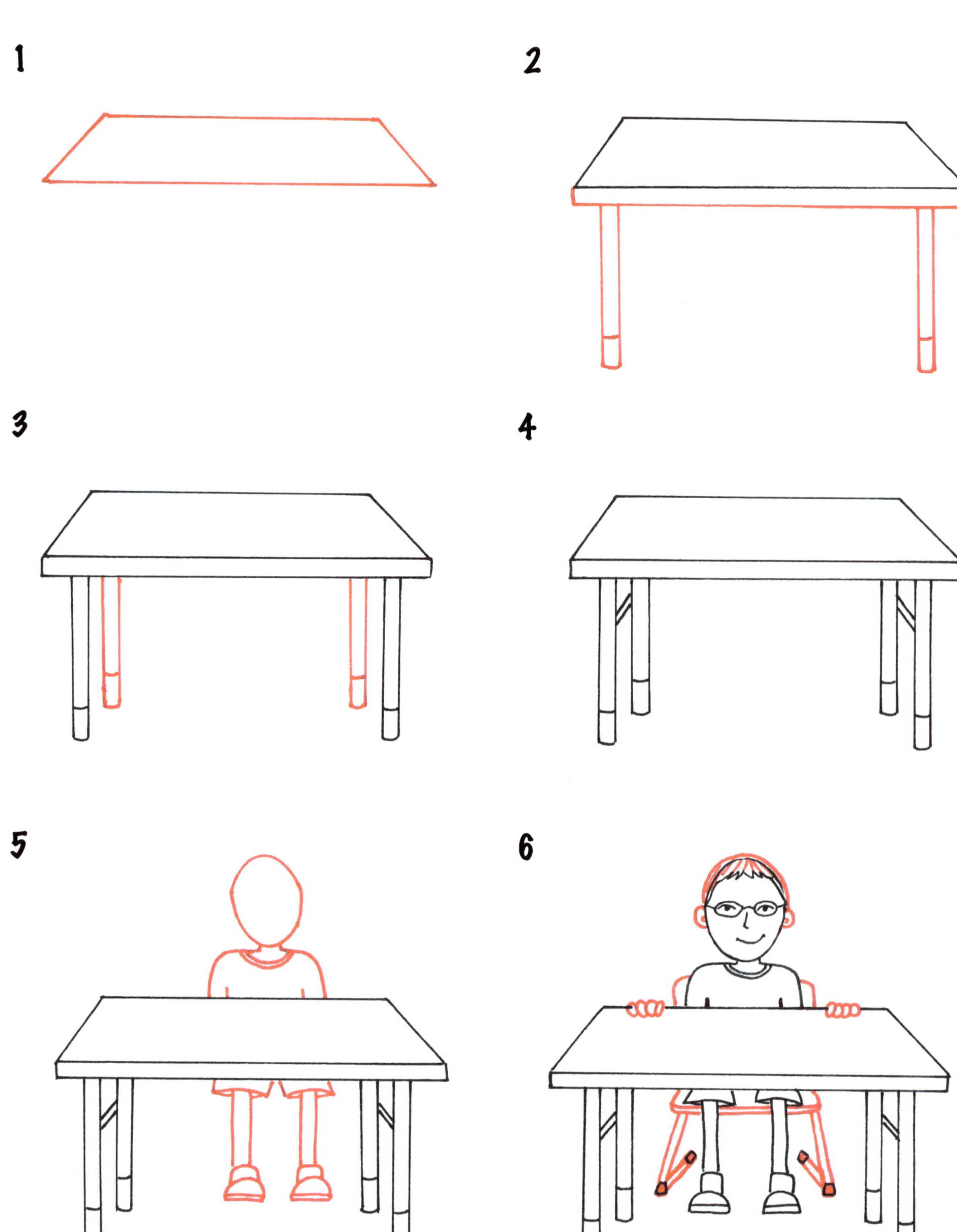

1

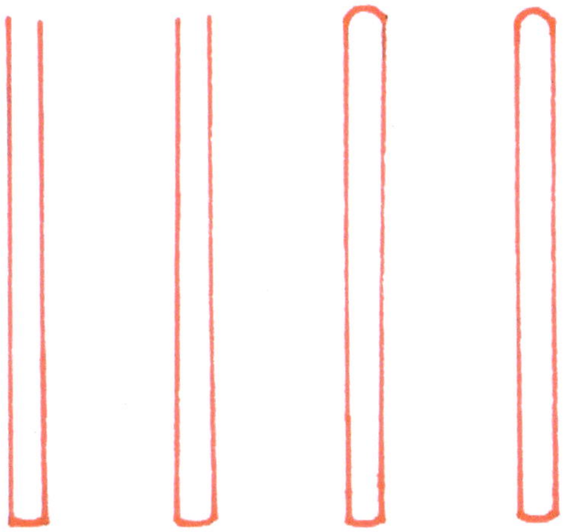

2

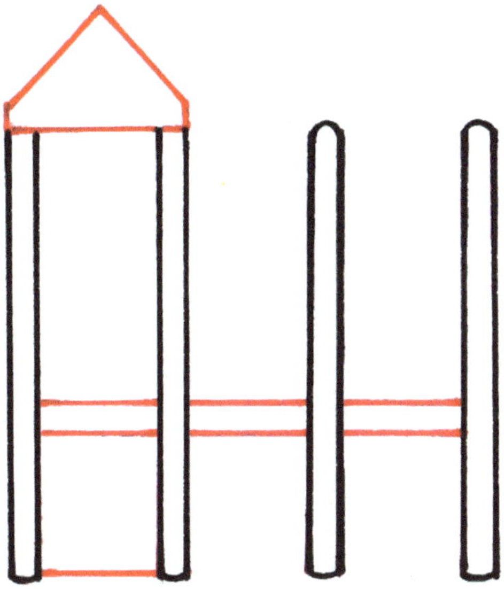

3

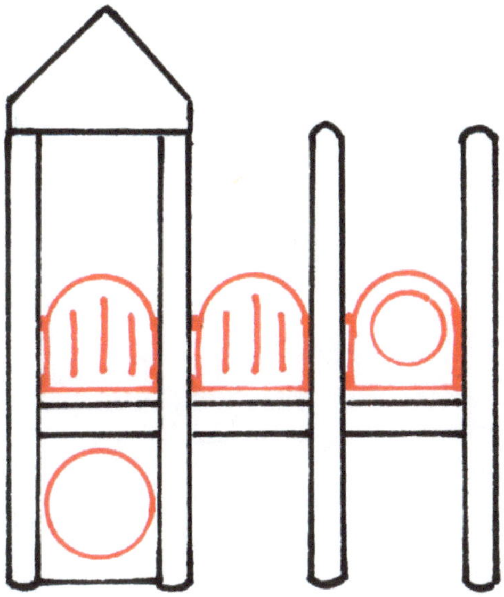

4

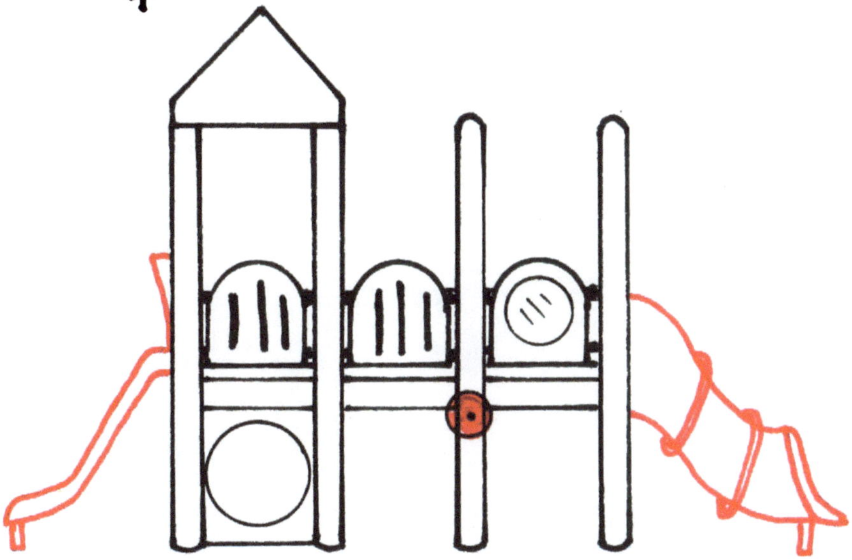

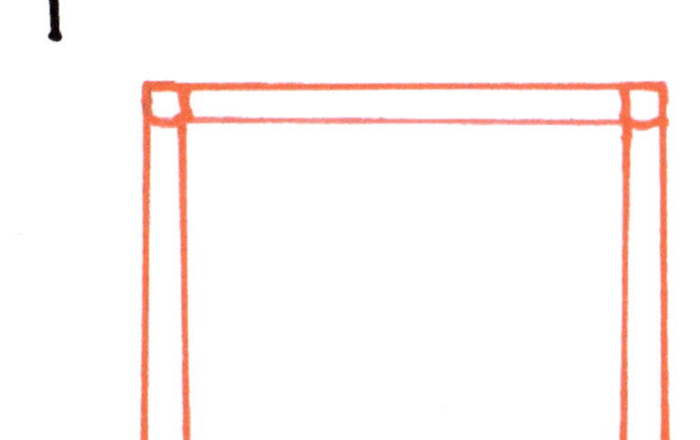

1

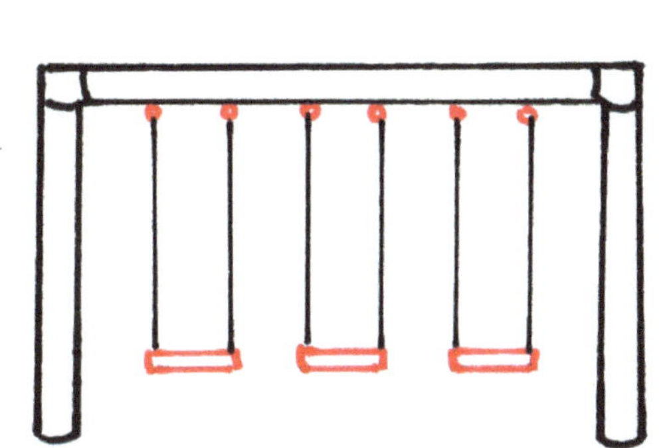

2

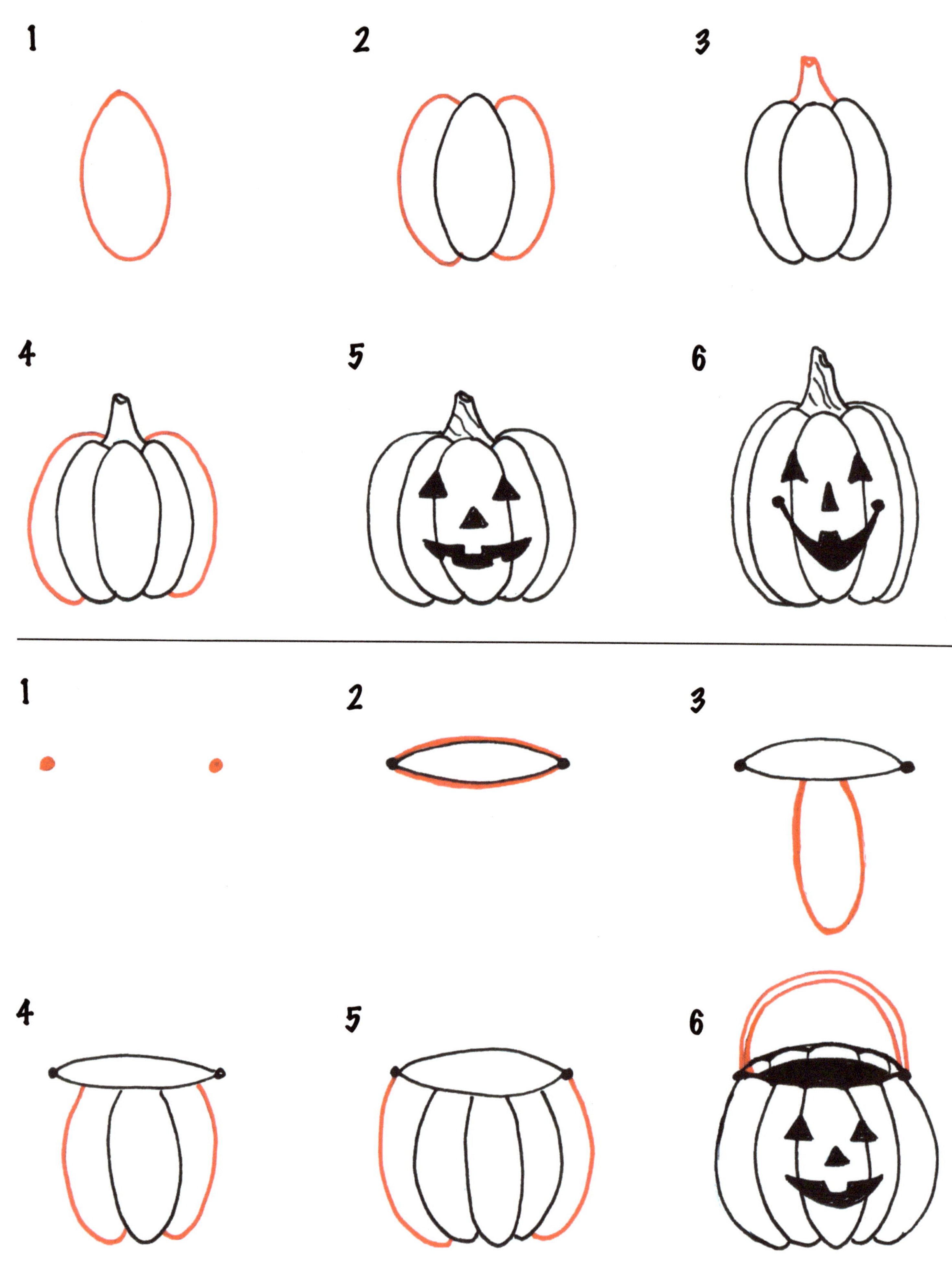

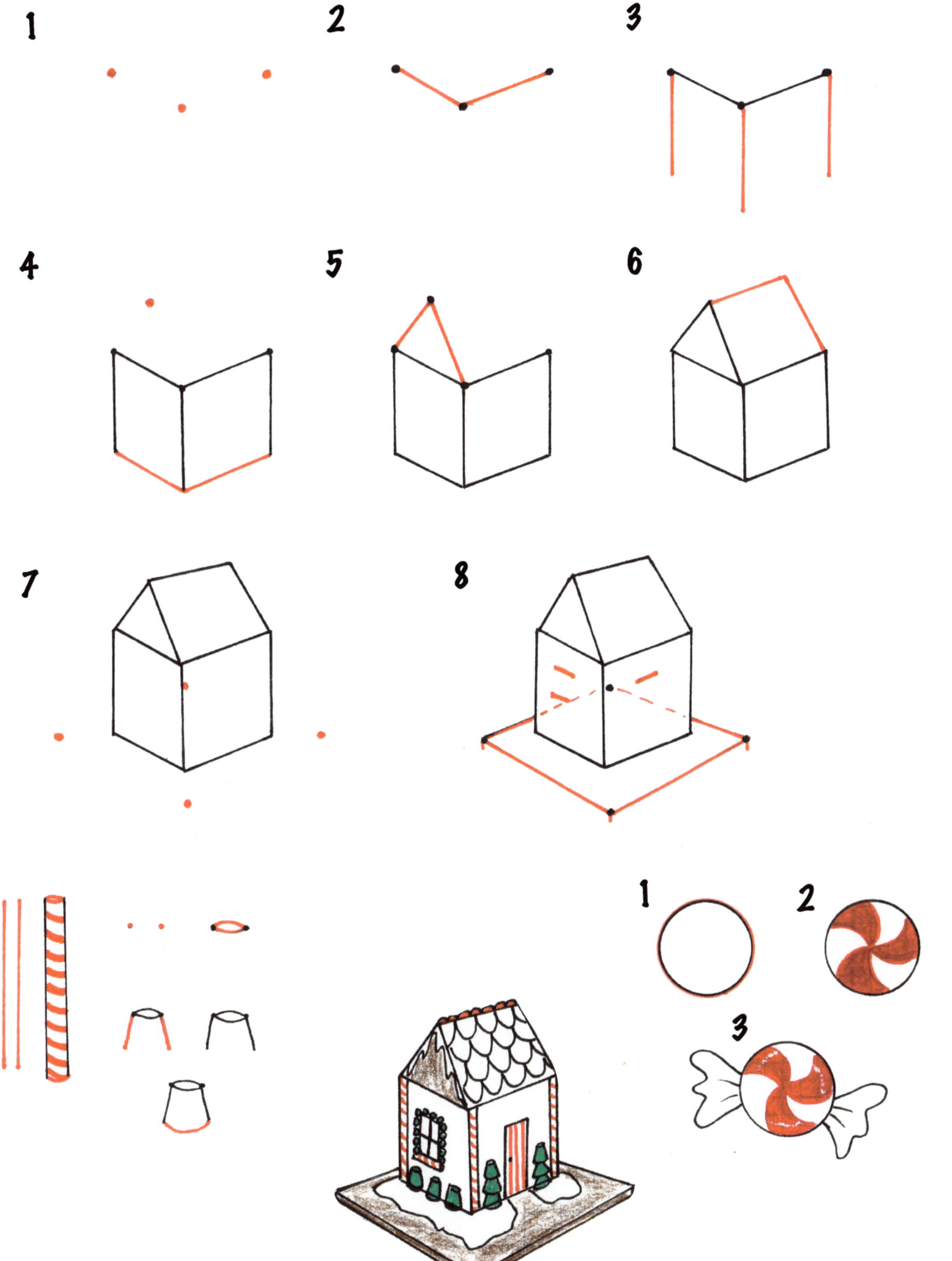

1
2
3
4
5
6
7
8
1
2
3

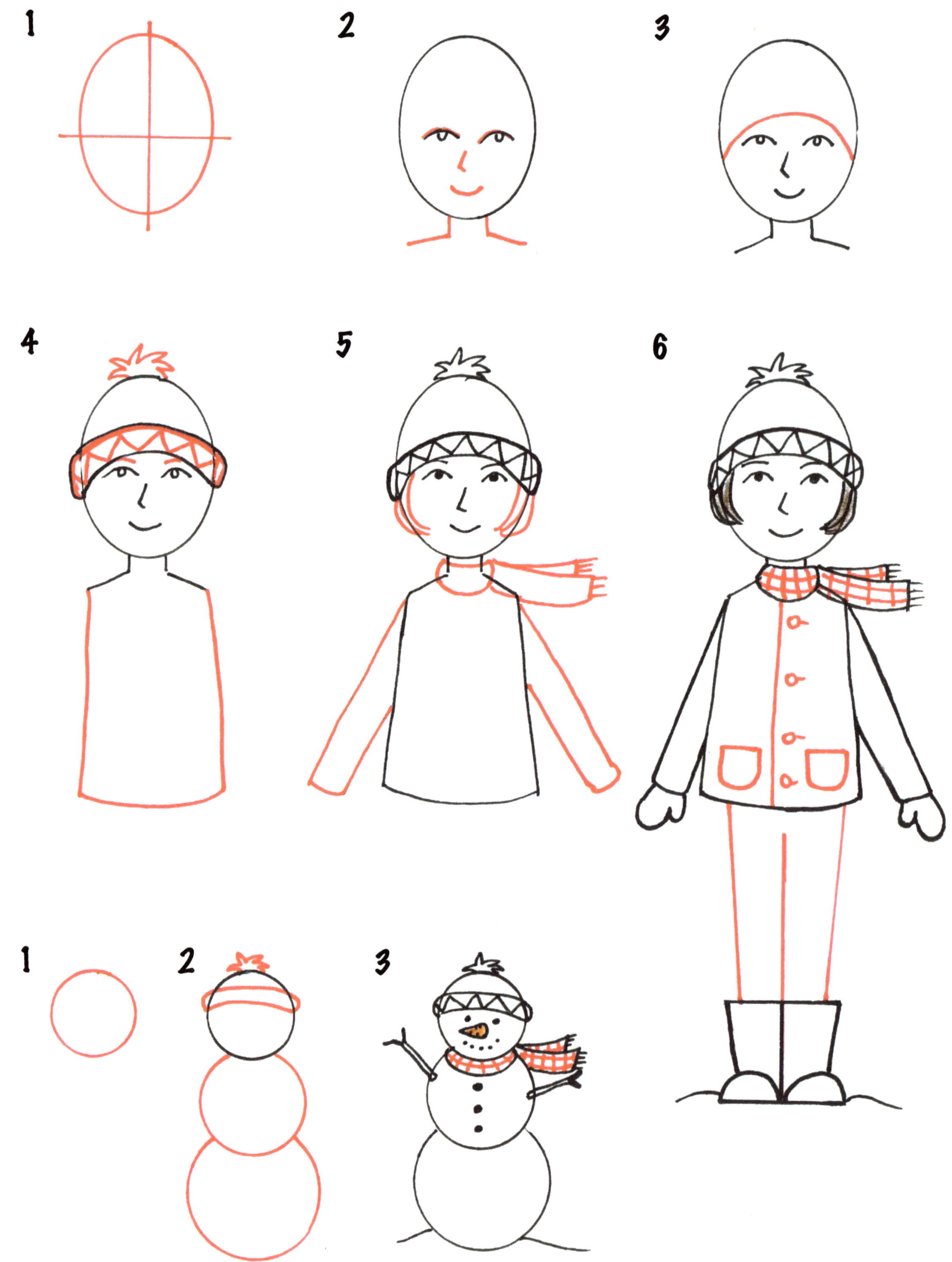

1
2
3
4
5
6
1
2
3

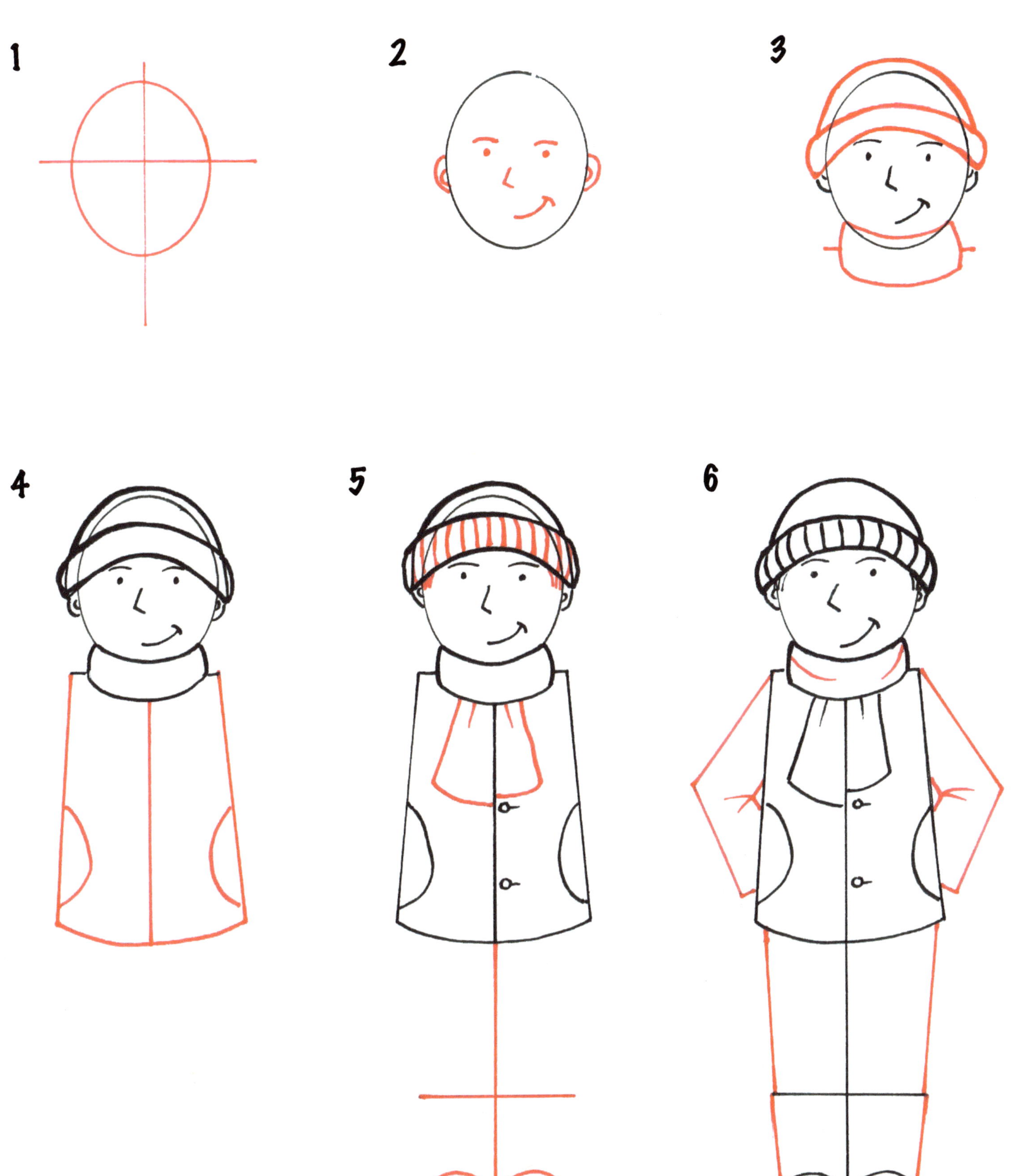

1
2
3
4
5
6

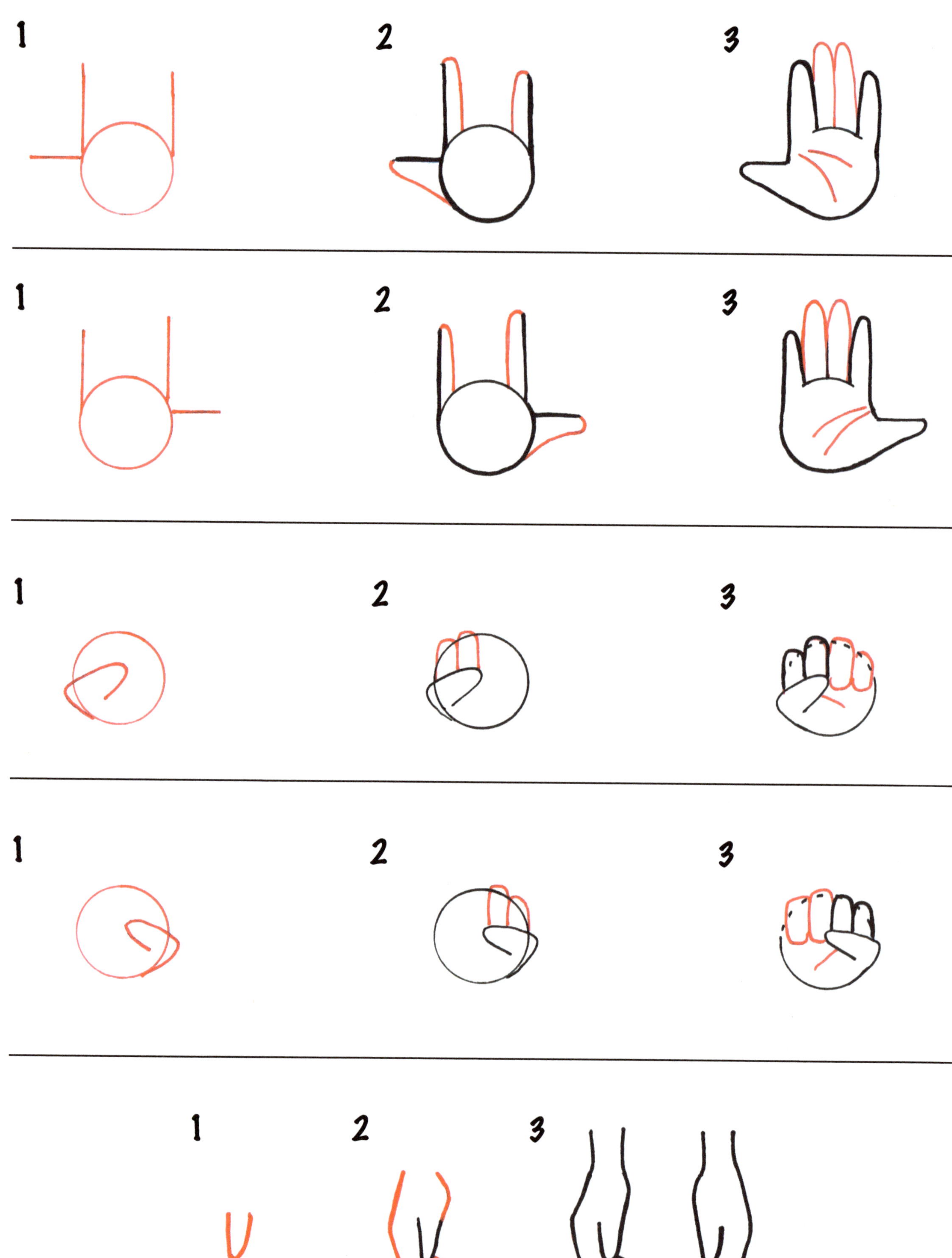

1
2
3

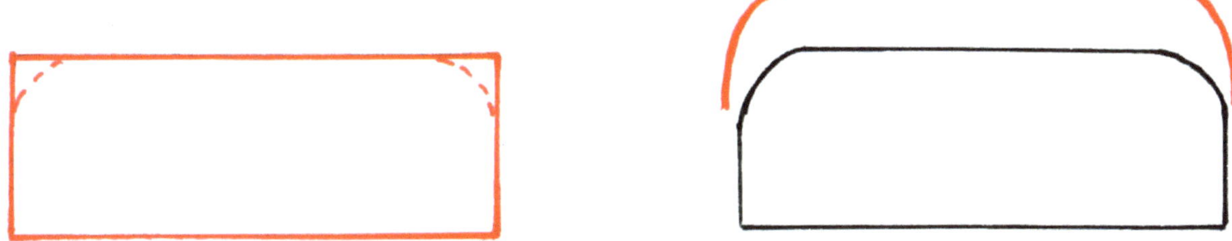

1
2
3
4

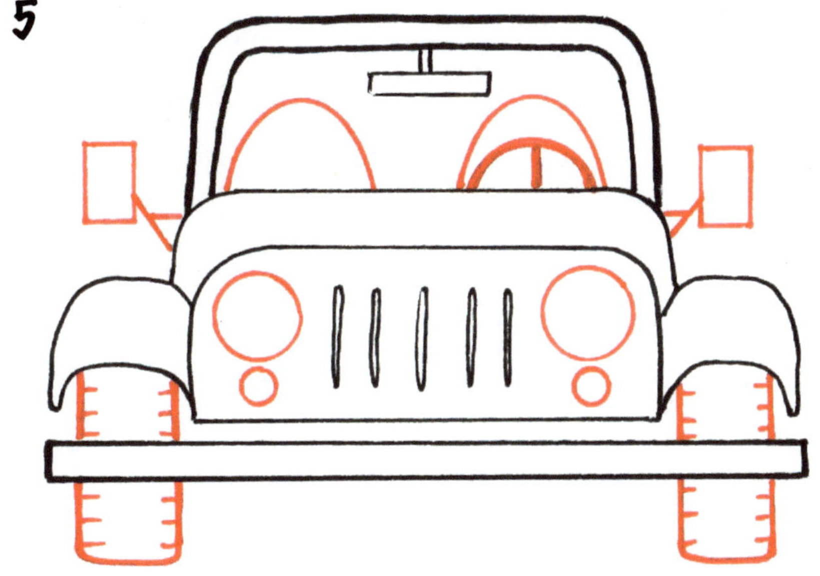

5

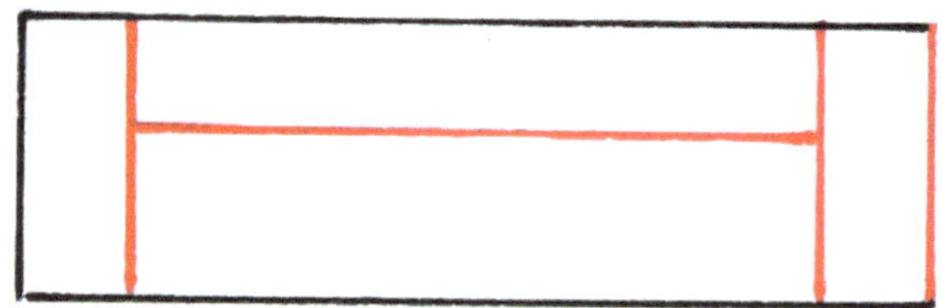

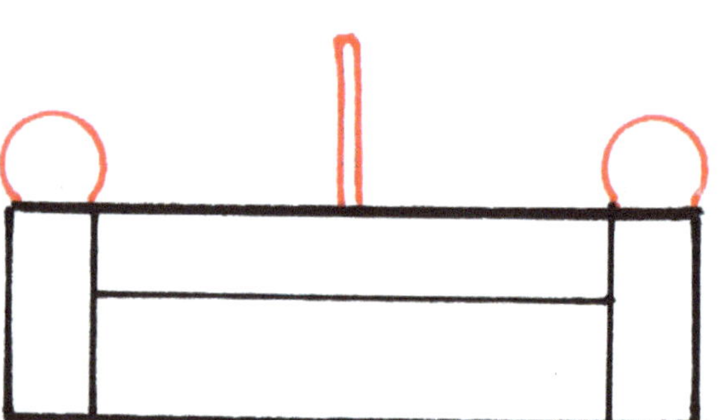

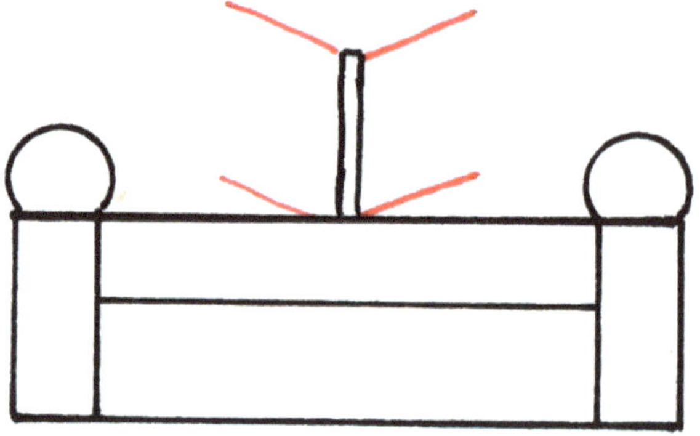

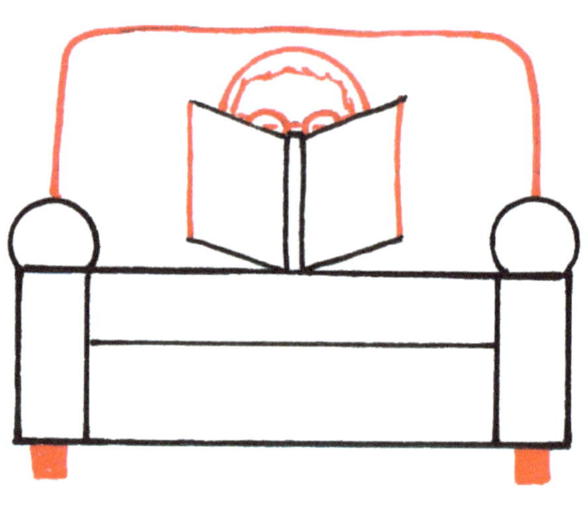

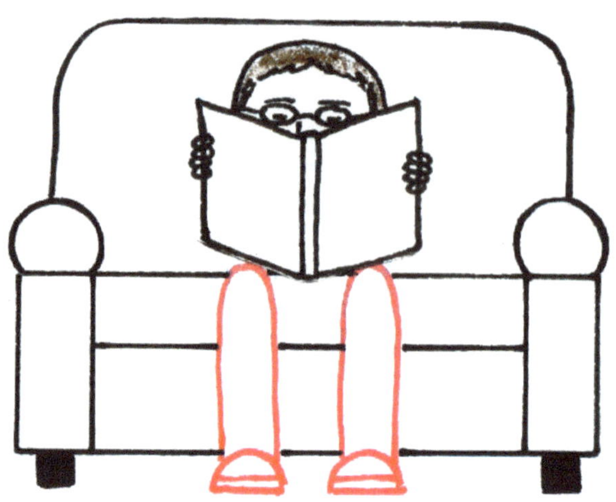

Student Art

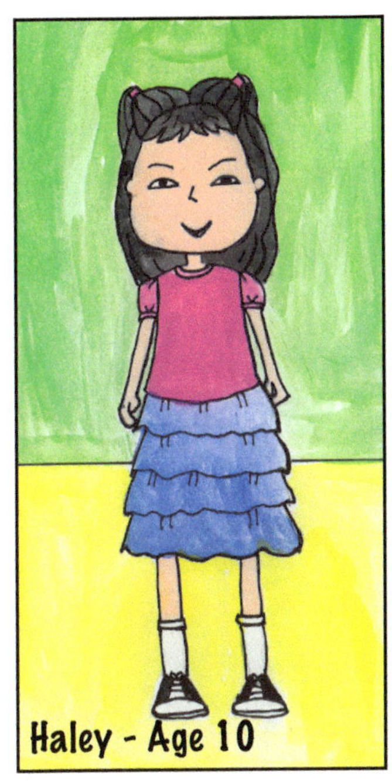

Haley - Age 10

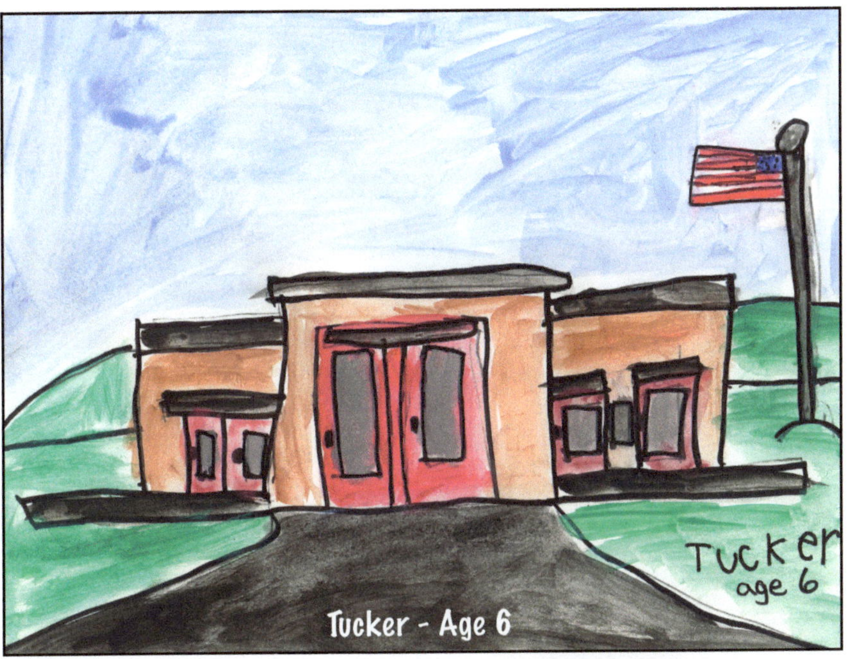

Tucker - Age 6

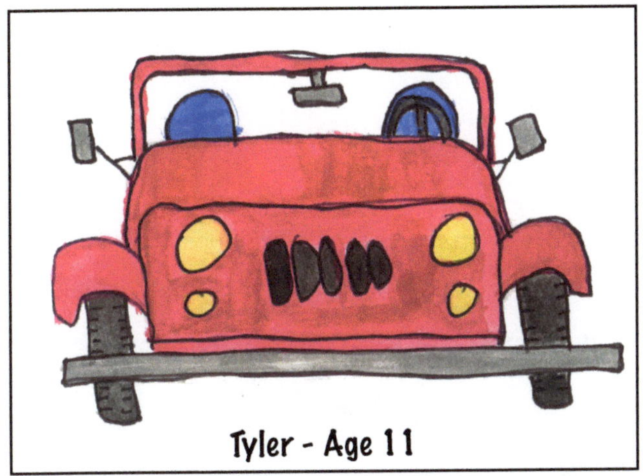

Tyler - Age 11

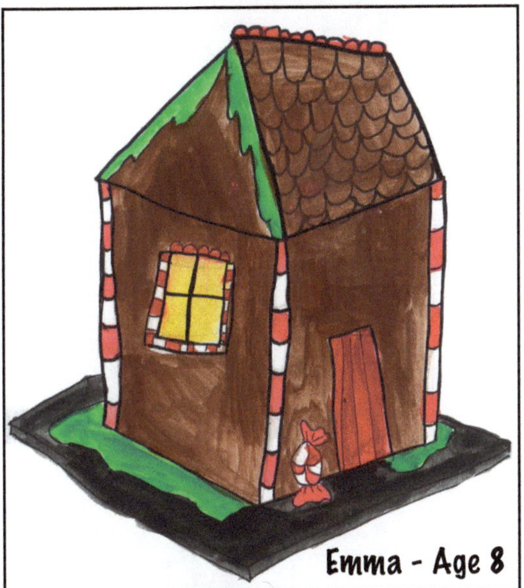

Emma - Age 8

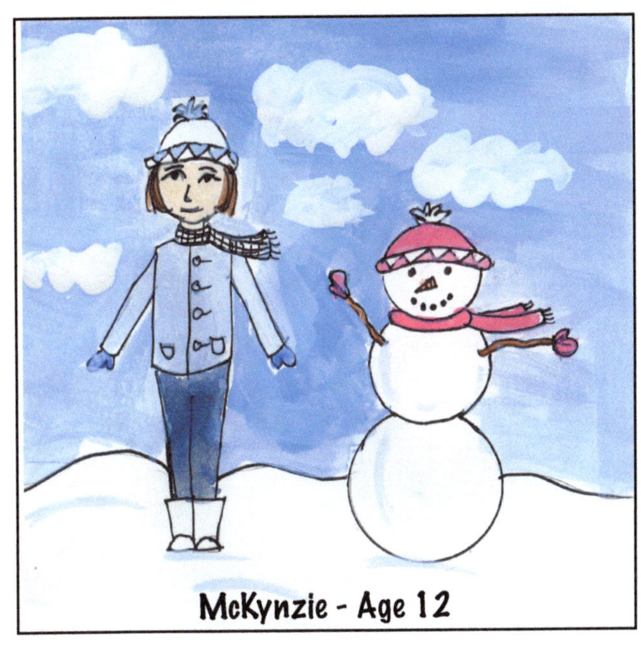

McKynzie - Age 12

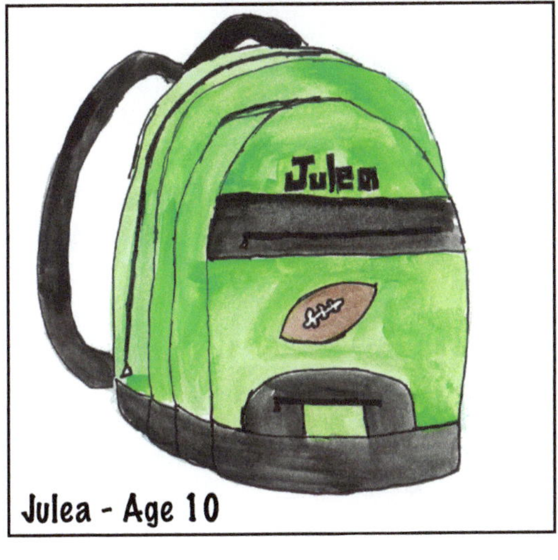

Julea - Age 10

Other books by Kaylea J. Mangrum

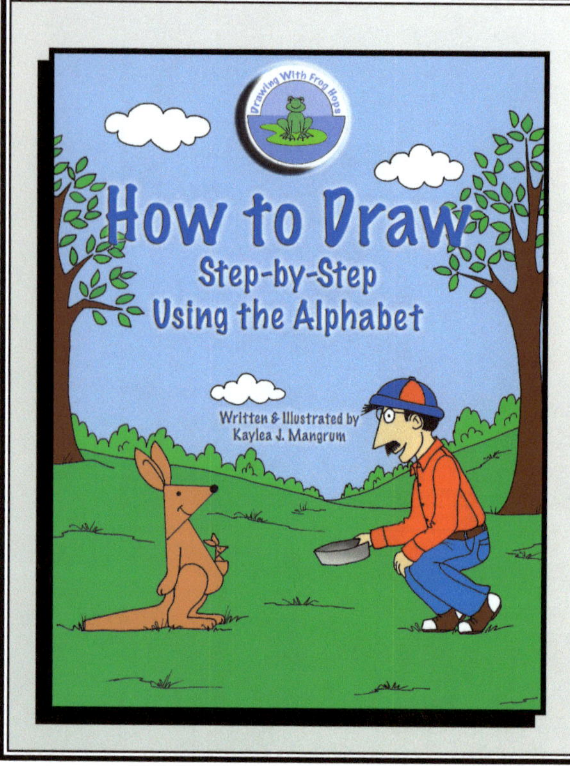

How to Draw Step-by-Step: Using the Alphabet

How to Draw Step-by-Step: With Special Kids

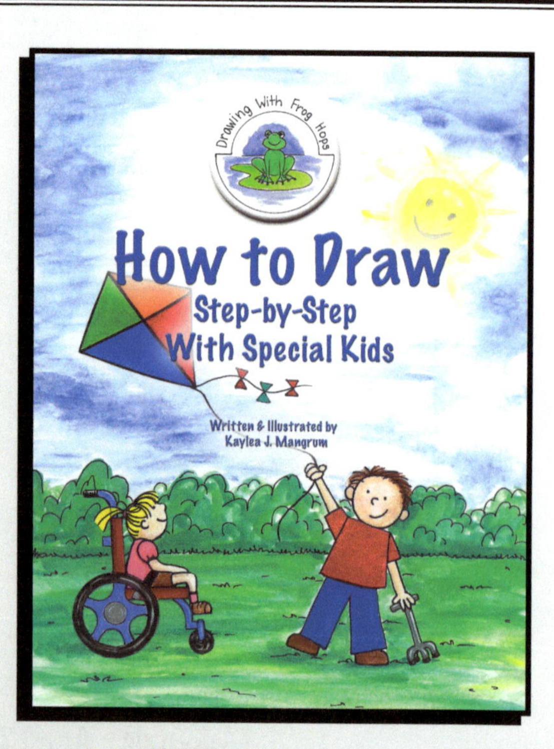